HOW TO READ
RAPHAEL'S
EPHEMERIS

JEFF MAYO
D.M.S. Astrol. (Hon.), D.F.Astrol.S.
Updated and Edited by Peter West

foulsham

LONDON • NEW YORK • TORONTO • SYDNEY

foulsham

The Publishing House, Bennetts Close,
Cippenham, Berks SL1 5AP

ISBN 0-572-02587-4

Page 94 reproduced, with permission, from data
supplied by HM Nautical Almanac Office © Particle
Physics and Astronomy Research Council.

Printed in Great Britain by St. Edmundsbury Press, Bury St. Edmunds, Suffolk

Foreword

An ephemeris is a book containing lists of astronomical data. Essentially, it provides the astrologer with the daily positions of the Sun, Moon and planets for one or more years, so that their positions can be calculated for any given time during that period.

The object of this book is to help the astrological student clearly understand, and make the fullest use of, all that is contained within the ephemeris. Several ephemerides are published annually in different countries, but there is no doubt that *Raphael's Ephemeris* is superior to all other publications and I highly recommend it. It is this excellent work that has been dissected here, with each page explained in detail.

On reading the title of this book, the average student may get the first impression that it can only be of interest to the beginner making initial contact with astrological factors and symbols. But this is not true.

In the simplest possible way, I have attempted to explain the various columns of data in the ephemeris, trying in a sense to view the apparent mass of figures and symbols through the eyes of the beginner so that even the factors most obvious to a trained astrologer are defined. However, I feel sure that there will be very many experienced students who will find much of value and enlightenment within these pages.

Raphael's Ephemeris has been published annually since 1821. Naturally, there have been periodical revisions and fresh data added. All data discussed here, therefore, has been taken from *Raphael's Astronomical Ephemeris of the Planets' Places for the Year 2000.*

The Symbols Employed

The Planets

☉	Sun	♃	Jupiter
☽	Moon	♄	Saturn
☿	Mercury	♅	Uranus
♀	Venus	♆	Neptune
⊕	Earth	♇	Pluto
♂	Mars		

The Zodiacal Signs

♈	Aries	♎	Libra
♉	Taurus	♏	Scorpio
♊	Gemini	♐	Sagittarius
♋	Cancer	♑	Capricorn
♌	Leo	♒	Aquarius
♍	Virgo	♓	Pisces

The Aspects

☌	0°	conjunction
●	0°	conjunction (occultation)
⩗	30° apart	semi-sextile
⊥	36° apart	semi-quintile
∠	45° apart	semi-square
⚹	60° apart	sextile
Q	72° apart	quintile
□	90° apart	square
△	120° apart	trine
⯒	135° apart	sesquiquadrate
±	144° apart	bi-quintile
▽	150° apart	quincunx (quincunc)
☍	180° apart	opposition
P (‖)	0°	parallel (in declination)

Solar Eclipse

☽☌☉ or ☽☌●

Lunar Eclipse

☽☍☉ or ☽☍☉

Nodes

☊ north node ☋ south node

The Mean Obliquity
of the Ecliptic

The mean obliquity of the ecliptic has been stated on the first page of *Raphael's Ephemeris* since 1904. This value is not used in the calculation of astrological charts, but the serious student will be interested to know what this information conveys to the trained astrologer.

The obliquity of the ecliptic means the oblique or slanting angle between the plane of the ecliptic and the plane of the equator, due to the tilt of the Earth's axis. The Earth's axis is slightly tilted, so that an angle is produced between the plane of the equator and the plane of the ecliptic. This is calculated using the Pole Star, or Polaris, which is slightly adrift of true north. Due to the precession of the equinoxes, this changes very slightly each year by about 50″ of arc in a retrograde motion. The obliquity is equal to the greatest distance from the equator reached by the Sun at the solstices, and it is measured in degrees, minutes and seconds of declination.

The mean (average) obliquity of the ecliptic for 2000 is 23° 26′ 21″. Fig. 8 on page 86 contains a table of astrological phenomena from *Raphael's Ephemeris*. Under the listings for June you may note that on 21 June at 01.48 am the Sun enters ♋ at the Summer Solstice. Under the column headed '⊙ Dec.' in Fig. 5 on page 83, you can see that the Sun's declination for 21 June is 23° 26′ N. The Sun has attained maximum declination north, its furthest angle from the equator during the year. The exact angle to a fraction of a second is not given, nor is such precision necessary for the astrologer's calculations.

Similarly, Fig. 8 tells us that the winter solstice occurs at 1.37 pm on 21 December. On 21 and 22 December the Sun's maximum declination is 23° 26′ S. For the second time in the year the Sun has reached its furthest distance (measured in declination) from the equator, but this time on the opposite side of the equator to its position in June.

The Sun's maximum declination at the solstices during June and December 2000 (23° 26') are the same, though less exactly given, as the value 23° 26' 21", or the mean obliquity of the ecliptic for 2000.

This value changes very, very gradually – a mere 47 seconds in 100 years. It is a subject to a cyclical change between the limits of 21° 59' and 24° 36'. The value at present is 23° 26'. At the rate of 47 seconds per century, it will be 11,000 to 12,000 years before the obliquity of the ecliptic has reached its lowest limit, 21° 59'. Over a period of 100 years the gradual change in the overall mean obliquity of the ecliptic has decreased by just 0.47".

Finding a
Planet's Position

The first section of *Raphael's Ephemeris* calculates the position of the Sun, the Moon and each planet for each day of the year, as measured in celestial longitude, declination and celestial latitude (except latitude for the Sun). The positions are calculated for noon Greenwich Mean Time (GMT).

In the ephemeris, two pages are allotted to each of the 12 months. Pages 2 and 3 from *Raphael's Ephemeris 2000* are reproduced on pages 79–80 in Figs. 1 and 2. These two pages give the most important planetary data for January 2000. If an astrologer is calculating a chart for a given time during January 2000, no matter where the birth or event occurred on the surface of the earth he has, by converting the local time to Greenwich Mean Time and referring to these pages, all the data required for finding the planet's positions for that given moment.

This data has not always been arranged exactly as shown on these pages. But once you know the symbols of the planets and which columns to look for on the monthly pages, you will easily be able to read these pages in earlier ephemerides.

To help you find the page in this book where you can read how to interpret the figures given for a particular planet's longitude, declination or latitude, the data referred to in Figs. 1 and 2 are listed in the indices on pages 12–13 (overleaf). For instance, if you want to know how to find the Moon's daily positions in declination and an explanation of what is meant by declination, you can refer to these indices. There you can read that the Moon's position for noon in declination can be found in column 8 of Fig. 1. Moreover, you can find an explanation of the Moon's declination on page 57.

Index for Fig. 1

Index for Fig. 2

Sidereal Time

Fig. 1 on page 79 is a reproduction of the left-hand page of *Raphael's Ephemeris* for January 2000. The page is divided into 11 columns. The first column gives the date of the month, with the letters D and M referring to the date and month respectively. The second column gives the days of the week, and the letters D and W refer to day and week respectively.

The third column refers to measurement in sidereal time. The letters H, M, S signify hours, minutes and seconds in sidereal time. For example, against 1 January we read 18.41.50. This is interpreted by the astrologer as 18 hours 41 minutes 50 seconds in sidereal time-reckoning.

To explain how this interpretation is arrived at, 18 is directly under the H (hours) and is read as 18 hours, 41 is directly under the M (minutes) and is read as 41 minutes, 50 is directly under the S (seconds) and is interpreted as 50 seconds. Thus, we have for 1 January the measurement 18H 41M 50S. But where is this measurement from and where is it going to?

First, we should know what is meant by sidereal time. This is a time system based on the true period of the earth's rotation on its axis. This rotation period is divided into exactly 24 sidereal hours. Sidereal derives from the Latin *sidus*, meaning 'star'. That is why sidereal time has been called 'time reckoned by the stars'.

We can understand this more clearly when we know that when a given star is chosen as a reference point, the period measured between two successive transits of this star over the observer's meridian will be exactly 24 sidereal hours in length. Sidereal time must not, however, be confused with clock time, which measures our day of 24 hours in terms of mean solar time. Mean solar time differs from sidereal time to the extent of approximately 3 minutes 56 seconds in every 24 hours (24 hours of mean solar time = 24 hours 3 minutes 56 seconds of sidereal time).

So now we know that the reading given for 1 January 2000 of 18H 41M 50S refers to a measurement based on the rotation of the

Earth on its axis. We will now be more precise. Once in every 24 sidereal hours the meridian of a given place (in this case, the Greenwich meridian) coincides with what is known as the First Point of Aries. The First Point of Aries is where the two great circles of ecliptic and equator intersect. The ecliptic is the apparent path of the Sun round the Earth, and it is only at the time of the vernal equinox that the Sun is exactly on this point of intersection. But the student must try to imagine the ecliptic as a path actually existing in the heavens, and in this way he will grasp that the First Point of Aries does not exist only at the time of the vernal equinox, but is in effect a reference point that can be employed as a basis for measurement at any moment of the year.

When, due to the rotation of the Earth on its axis, the First Point of Aries crosses (transits) the meridian of a given place, measurement in sidereal time for that given place begins. The moment the First Point of Aries again transits the meridian, one sidereal day, or a period of exactly 24 hours of sidereal time, has elapsed, and a new sidereal day begins. Measurement in sidereal time is westwards along the equator. Thus, when we read that on 1 January 2000 at noon for Greenwich the sidereal time is 18H 41M 50S, this tells us that measurement in sidereal time in a westward direction along the equator the First Point of Aries is 18 hours 41 minutes 50 seconds. In other words, this is the period that has elapsed in terms of sidereal time (not clock time) since the First Point of Aries was exactly on the Greenwich meridian.

We have said that sidereal time differs from clock time (mean solar time) by an average excess of 3 minutes 56 seconds of sidereal time. This is clearly shown by the sidereal time figures in the third column of Fig. 1. The figures increase daily by almost (or exactly) 3 minutes 56 seconds. If we subtract 18H 41M 50S (for 1 January) from 18H 45M 47S (for 2 January) we find that the increase between the two days is 3 minutes 57 seconds. If we subtract 18H 45M 47S (2 January) from 18H 49M 44S (3 January), we find the increase between them is 3 minutes 57 seconds.

You can go on doing this for consecutive days right through the year, and you will arrive at the same average increase in sidereal time over the 24-hour period of mean solar time between two consecutive noons at Greenwich. But this increase does not mean that the Earth only turns on its axis a mere 3 minutes 56 seconds between two consecutive noons. In a period of 24 hours clock time, the Earth turns on its axis a full 24 hours 3 minutes 56 seconds of sidereal time.

The Sun's Longitude and Declination

The position of the Sun in celestial longitude will be found on the left-hand page for each month in *Raphael's Ephemeris*, in the fourth column (headed '⊙ Long.'). The left-hand page for January is reproduced from *Raphael's Ephemeris 2000* in Fig. 1 on page 79.

Celestial longitude is measurement along the ecliptic eastwards from the First Point of Aries, as viewed from the Earth, and is given for noon at Greenwich for each day of the month.

Measurement is in degrees (°), minutes (′) and seconds (″) of arc. Unless a very precise measurement is required of the Sun's position at a given time, you need only use degrees and minutes for the normal birth chart calculation. When seconds exceed 30″, these can be converted into one whole minute and added to the minutes given. For example, the Sun's position at noon on 1 January is 10° 22′ 8″ Capricorn (♑). As 22′ 8″ is less than 30′, we may safely say that the Sun's position is 10° ♑, to the nearest whole degree. On 9 January, the position of the Sun is 18° 31′ 32″ of the same sign, Capricorn. To the nearest whole degree, this may be read as 19° ♑.

When taking down the position of the Sun or a planet from *Raphael's Ephemeris,* do not automatically assume that it is in the sign given at the top of the column against the first day of the month. For instance, the Sun is in Capricorn (♑) on 1 January 2000, but a new sign (♒) is shown against 21 January. If you note carefully the Sun's noon positions on 20 and 21 January you will see that the Sun enters ♒ after midday on the 20 January, though at noon on that date it is still in ♑ – only just, by a mere 14″.

In the fifth column on the left-hand page for each month we can find the co-ordinate referring to declination with respect to the Sun. The column is headed '⊙ Dec.'. Declination refers to the distance in degrees and minutes that a celestial body is north or south of the Earth's equator. The equator is the natural zero for declination, and when the Sun is exactly on the plane of the equator as viewed from the Earth (which occurs at the equinoxes) it has declination 0°.

However, in the case of the Sun, declination is actually the measured distance between the Sun's centre and the Earth's equator at the point on the Earth's surface facing the Sun. It is not the Sun that has risen or fallen in its orbit by anything up to 23.5°, but the changing position of the Earth relative to the Sun that determines the Sun's declination.

We see, therefore, the declination measurements given in column five in Fig. 1 as being connected with the Earth–Sun system. For example, the Sun's declination on 1 January 2000 is 23° 2' S, which tells us that the Sun is then 23° 2' south of the Earth's equator.

The Moon's Longitude and Declination

The Moon's Longitude

Under the heading '☽ Long.', in the sixth column of the left-hand page for each month, is given the celestial longitude of the Moon in degrees (°), minutes (′) and seconds (″) of arc. Measurement is eastwards along the ecliptic from the First Point of Aries.

The Moon, as a satellite of the Earth, and therefore being considerably nearer to our planet compared to the immense distances separating us from the other planets, moves with relative rapidity through the 12 signs of the zodiac. Indeed, the Moon takes an average of just under 27.5 days (a sidereal month) to complete the 360° circle of the zodiac, as viewed from the Earth. Compare this with the Sun's 365 days, or the 88 days of Mercury, the planet nearest to the Sun, or 248 years of Pluto, the furthest known planet from the Sun. The Moon takes an average of less than 2.5 days to pass through one sign.

Referring to Fig. 1 on page 79, we note that for noon at Greenwich on 1 January 2000 the Moon is in ♏ 13° 19′ 26″. As was mentioned in the case of the Sun, for ordinary natal chart calculations measurement to precise seconds can be ignored when less than 30″. If it is given as 30″ or over, then one whole minute can be added to the given minutes. In the above example, the 26″ can therefore be ignored.

When the Moon changes signs, the new sign is only entered against the date if this occurs before noon. The actual times when the Moon enters each sign is referred to in Fig. 11 on page 89.

The Moon's Declination

The eighth column of Fig. 1 gives the Moon's position in declination at noon in Greenwich. (See the explanation of declination on page 19.)

The capital S at the top of this column, between the figures 10 and 54, means south. Further down the column (against the eighth day of the month) we find another capital S, which tells us that at noon for Greenwich on 1 January 2000 the Moon is in declination south. Its position measured southwards from the celestial equator is then 10° 54′.

For each successive day until the N is shown, the Moon is in south declination. It would be rather pointless to denote N or S for every day, as we can see more clearly whether declination is north or south when this is only indicated for the noon *after* the Moon has crossed the equator.

The only exception to the rule that N or S is stated on the day the Moon crosses the equator, is that for the first day of each month we are shown whether the Moon is in north or south declination. This rule applies also to the Sun's declination, and to the latitude of the Moon and to the latitude and declination of the planets.

Increase and Decrease in Declination

The Moon (or Sun or planet) is said to be increasing in declination when it is moving in the direction (north or south, as the case may be) from the equator towards maximum declination. As the term implies, the measurement of the distance between the Moon and the equator increases each successive day. As an example, the Moon is increasing in declination between 1 and 6 January (Fig. 1).

We can find out whether the Moon has actually reached maximum declination south before or after noon on 6 January by referring to the section headed Phenomena 2000 in Fig. 8 on page 86. At the top of the page it is stated that at 9.41 am on 6 January the Moon is at maximum declination 20° 57′ S. Turning to Fig. 1 again, we note the Moon's declination at noon on 6 January is 20° 57′ S.

From the moment the Moon has reached maximum declination it is said to be decreasing in declination, and at each successive noon its distance from the equator will be less. Its motion in declination is then from maximum north or south towards the equator. As an example, between 6 and 12 January (Fig. 1) the Moon's declination is decreasing. As we found in Fig. 8 (see page 86), maximum declination north is at 9.41 am on 6 January. That is when the Moon's declination begins to decrease, until some time around 13–14 January, when the Moon crosses the equator from south to north.

When Is the Moon on the Equator?

Do we know exactly when the Moon is on the equator? Yes, by turning again to the Phenomena section (Fig. 8). Near the top of the page we can read that at 3.38 pm on 13 January the Moon is on the equator. You may wonder why the letter N (indicating change of direction from south to north declination) is not given for 13 January, the day when the equator is crossed. The reason is that at noon on the 13 January the Moon is still south of the equator. But by noon on the following day, 14 January, the Moon has reached a distance of 4° 2′ N, and so the letter N must now be entered to show that these figures are to be read for north declination.

An Important Rule When Calculating

When the time of a given birth is known, and calculation is required to find the exact degree and minute of declination the Moon occupies at that moment, you need to be careful to note whether the Moon is increasing or decreasing in declination. The rule to follow is this:

- When birth time (GMT) is **am** and declination is **increasing**, the interval motion in declination must be **subtracted** from the noon position.
- When birth time (GMT) is **am** and declination is **decreasing**, the interval motion in declination must be **added** to the noon position.
- When birth time (GMT) is **pm** and declination is **increasing**, the interval motion in declination must be **added** to the noon position.
- When birth time (GMT) is **pm** and declination is **decreasing**, the interval motion in declination must be **subtracted** from the noon position.

Interval motion refers to the motion in declination of the Moon from birth time to noon (for an am birth), or from noon to birth time (for a pm birth). This rule applies to the declination motion of each planet and the Sun. However, in the Moon's case, where the daily motion can be so much greater than with the other planets, so can a larger error be made if this rule is not observed.

Maximum Declination Affected by Latitude

If you look through several ephemerides for consecutive years you will notice that the Moon's maximum declination varies from month to month, and year to year. Over a period of 19 years the Moon's maximum declination will have reached at one stage in this cycle a 'high' of around 28° 35′, and at another and opposite stage in the cycle a 'low' of about 18° 19′.

The reason for this is the phenomenon known as the regression of the nodes, coupled to the angle of the Moon's orbit to the ecliptic (latitude). The zodiac is the belt, or path, of the Sun known as the ecliptic. It is located in the heavens and extends by about 8° north and south of its centre. As it is the Sun's path, the Sun can never travel outside it. However, it does move daily from one side of this pathway to the other. This movement is known as declination north or south.

The maximum declination north, which is about 23.5°, is reached at the summer solstice in the northern hemisphere. Maximum declination south is at the winter solstice. The Moon's orbit carries it at a slight angle to the ecliptic. The two points where the Moon cuts the plane of the ecliptic are known as the nodes. The ascending node is called the Dragon's Head, the descending node is the Dragon's Tail.

Referring to the data listed in Fig. 8 on page 86, we can note, for instance, the variation in the maximum distance from the equator attained by the Moon in terms of south declination during the first six months of 2000.

6 January	20° S 57′	
2 February	20° S 56′	
29 February	21° S 01′	
28 March	21° S 13′	
24 April	21° S 29′	
21 May	21° S 40′	
18 June	21° S 45′	and so on …

The Moon's Longitude and Declination for Midnight (00h 00m)
In the tenth and eleventh columns of Fig. 2 on page 80 are given the positions of the Moon in celestial longitude and declination for midnight at the end of the day. In the old days an astrologer would rarely have used this information. Many modern astrologers do make use of this data but would look to an ephemeris that lists the individual planetary positions for midnight, or 00 hours 00 minutes.

It is quite easy to calculate the midnight positions from *Raphael's Ephemeris* and this is dealt with in the chapter on calculations on page 75.

The Moon's Latitude and Nodes

The Moon's Latitude

The Moon's position in terms of celestial latitude is given in the seventh column of the left-hand page for each month (see Fig. 1 on page 79). The latitude of the Moon refers to measurement of its position north or south of the ecliptic, in degrees and minutes of arc. A planet's latitude is similarly measured. The Sun cannot have latitude, as the plane of the great circle of the ecliptic passes through the centres of both the Sun and the Earth.

The Moon's latitude is not normally used by astrologers in their natal chart calculations. It is interesting, however, to learn something of the significance of the Moon's latitude in the scheme of the celestial patterns. Latitude is measurement of the Moon's orbital inclination. The figures given for a particular day at noon tell us how the Moon's orbit is tilted relative to the plane of the ecliptic. The maximum angle of tilt is 5° 18′ and the mean tilt is 5° 8′. By following the increase and decrease in latitude as indicated by the figures in the seventh column of Fig. 1, we can see a connection between latitude and the nodal motion of the Moon.

The Moon's Nodes

The nodes are the points of intersection of the Moon's orbit of the Earth and the great circle of the ecliptic (the Earth's orbit of the Sun). At the top of the page from *Raphael's Ephemeris* reproduced in Fig. 1 is a column headed '☽ Node'. This refers to the Moon's north node, which is the point in the ecliptic where the Moon in its orbit crosses the ecliptic from south to north.

We can check this if we refer again to the Moon's latitude (see Fig. 1). On 1 January, the Moon's latitude is given as 5° 10′ north of the ecliptic. At noon on 2 January, the Moon's latitude has decreased to 4° 53′ N. By noon on 3 January, latitude is 4° 23′ N. Then by noon on 8 January, the letter S appears, indicating that the Moon crosses the ecliptic from north to south. Thus, on 8 January the Moon, in its path around the Earth, reaches its south node.

To enable us to interpret the Moon's data more clearly, the ninth column provides us with figures for the Moon's north node. On 8 January the Moon's latitude changes from north to south when the Moon, as it crosses the ecliptic, reaches its south node. Checking with the north node's column of figures in Fig. 1, note that the point on the ecliptic occupied by the node is ♌ 4° 40′.

When the Moon crosses the ecliptic in the opposite direction, from north to south, we find the Moon's longitude on that day to be in the opposite sign to that of the north node. This is because the Moon will then be at its south node. If we refer to the Moon's latitude again (seventh column) we see that at noon on 8 January the Moon's position is 0° 16′ S. On the previous day, 7 January, the Moon's latitude is still north of the ecliptic at 0° 50′ N. This is further away from the ecliptic (0°) than is 0° 16′, and so it follows that it is on 8 January and not 7 January when the Moon reaches its south node. The north node's position on the ecliptic at noon on 7 January is ♌ 4° 44′ (Fig. 1). We shall, therefore, expect to find that during 7 January the Moon is in the opposite sign to Leo (♌) which is Aquarius (♒). At noon on 7 January the Moon is in Leo (♌) 4° 44′; at midnight (tenth column) in Aquarius (♒) 0° 34′. Thus, during the morning of 8 January the Moon reached its south node.

The Longitude of
the Planets

The first column in the upper portion of Fig. 2 on page 80 refers to the date in the month. The next eight headings refer to the daily positions of the eight planets used in astrology: Mercury, Venus, Mars, Jupiter, Saturn, Uranus, Neptune and Pluto. As indicated by the abbreviation 'Long.' under the glyph for each planet at the head of the columns, these positions refer to measurement in celestial longitude. Celestial longitude is measurement along the ecliptic eastwards from the First Point of Aries, as viewed from the Earth. It is given here for noon at Greenwich for each day of the month. Measurement is in degrees (°) and minutes (').

The Longitude of Mercury (☿)

Mercury is the planet nearest to the Sun, and its daily positions in longitude are given in the upper second column (Fig. 2). Being also relatively close to the Earth, Mercury is seen (from the standpoint of the Earth) moving rapidly for most of the year, at times over 2° in one day.

Referring to Fig. 2, we can see that Mercury is placed in two zodiacal signs during January 2000. Between 1 and 18 January it is in Capricorn (♑) and between 19 and 31 January it is passing through Aquarius (♒). One must be careful to notice when a planet changes signs, and not simply take it to still be in the sign that appears at the top of the column.

The Longitude of Venus (♀)

Venus is the planet second in order from the Sun, and its daily positions in longitude for noon at Greenwich are given in the upper third column. In Fig. 2, Venus is shown as moving through Sagittarius (♐). Venus passes from Sagittarius to enter Capricorn (♑) on 24 January.

The Longitude of Mars (♂)

Mars is the planet fourth in order from the Sun, and its daily positions in longitude are shown in the upper fourth column (see Fig. 2 on page 80). Mars is shown moving through Aquarius (≈) for the first three days of January, entering Pisces (⟩⟨) at 03h 01m on the fourth day of the month.

Mars is a great deal nearer the Earth than is Jupiter (Earth being the planet third in order from the Sun, and therefore 'next' to Mars), which means that when Mars is moving at its fastest along the ecliptic it may cover a distance of 48′ in a period of 24 hours. Thus, unless Mars is close to its stationary point and can be noted through consecutive days' positions to be moving very slowly, a calculator should be used to determine its exact position for a given time of day. One then turns to Daily Motions of the Planets (see Fig. 6 on page 84) for the particular month to find the motion of Mars during the respective 24-hour period to be used in calculations. (See The Daily Motion of Mars, page 55.)

The Longitude of Jupiter (♃)

Jupiter is the planet fifth in order from the Sun, and its longitude is given in the upper fifth column of Fig. 2. This fairly slow-moving giant is shown travelling from 25° 15′ Aries (♈) on 1 January, through to 27° 53′ of the same sign on 31 January. At its fastest, Jupiter travels about 12′ along the ecliptic in a period of 24 hours, as seen from the Earth.

The Longitude of Saturn (♄)

Saturn is the planet sixth in order from the Sun and its longitude is given in the upper sixth column (Fig. 2). Saturn starts the month in 10° 24′ Taurus (♉) but, if you look carefully, immediately underneath this data is a capital letter R, which means the planet's movement is retrograde. On the following day, its position is slightly less than the first day because it appears to be moving backwards. Also, when we read the consecutive days' positions, we note the figures are decreasing and that the planet is gradually slowing, until, on the tenth day, the planet does, in fact, seem to be standing still.

On the twelfth day you see that a D has been placed alongside the degrees. This shows that the planet is now stationary but will start to move 'direct', that is, forwards again. By the end of the month, Saturn has reached 10° 38′ in the sign of Taurus. Because it was in retrograde motion, became stationary, and then started to move forward, it has, throughout January, only moved a total of 14′ from 10° 24′ Taurus on the first day to 10° 38′ Taurus on the last day. In this particular instance Saturn originally became retrograde on Monday 30 August 1999 at 1.34 am.

Thus, throughout September, October, November and December, and until Wednesday 12 January, Saturn will appear to be moving backwards for a total of 135 days. In terms of secondary progressions (where one ephemeris day is equal to one year of life), Saturn could be retrograde throughout the entire lifetime of an individual.

The Longitude of Uranus (♅)

Uranus is the planet seventh in order from the Sun. The longitudinal position of Uranus appears in the upper seventh column, and the sign at the top of the column (♒) shows that this planet is in Aquarius.

This is a very slow-moving planet and only travels a few minutes per day. It begins the month at 14° 49′ Aquarius and has only reached 16° 28′ Aquarius by the month's end, which amounts to an average movement of about three minutes (3′) per day.

The Longitude of Neptune (♆)

Neptune is the eighth planet in order from the Sun, the second most distant in our solar system. Neptune's longitude appears in the upper eighth column. There is never the need to calculate this planet's position for a given time, since its daily motion is negligible. During January 2000, Neptune attains a maximum daily motion of a mere 2′ on only seven days. For instance, between noon on 3 January (3° 16′) and noon on 4 January (3° 18′), a forward or direct motion along the ecliptic of 2′ (see Fig. 2). Neptune is shown in the sign Aquarius by the glyph (♒) against the first of the month.

The Longitude of Pluto (♇)

Pluto is the ninth planet in order from the Sun, the most distant in our solar system. Pluto's longitude is in the upper ninth column of Fig. 2. Like Neptune, there is never a need to calculate Pluto's precise position, since it moves about two minutes (2′) per day. Occasionally, it may move three minutes, while at other times there may only be one minute from one day to the next. For examples of this look to the difference in positions between 4 and 5 January and between 30 and 31 January. In 2000 Pluto moves from 11° 27′ Sagittarius on 1 January to only 12° 21′ Sagittarius on 31 January.

The Declination and Latitude of the Planets

Declination

Declination refers to the angular distance a planet is north or south of the celestial equator. This angle is measured in degrees (°) and minutes (′) from the plane of the equator (dec. 0°).

In the bottom sections of the left- and right-hand pages for each month in *Raphael's Ephemeris* (Figs. 1 and 2 on pages 79 and 80) are the declinations for each of the planets. These begin with Mercury and end with Pluto in the respective columns headed 'Dec.'. The dates for these positions at noon at Greenwich are given in the first column, under the heading 'DM'.

The positions for Mercury, Venus and Mars are given for noon at Greenwich for each day of the month, because the motion of these three planets in declination carries them quite a distance in a period of 24 hours (except when around maximum declination). With Mercury, in particular, it might become necessary to use a calculator should you wish to establish its precise declination for a given time. There are two columns for declination for these three planets. In Fig. 1 we read that on 1 January Mercury is in 24° 25′ south declination. In the next column on the right, half a line lower, you will see that Mercury's declination is 24° 29′ S, which is its position for noon at Greenwich on 2 January. Returning to the first of the two declination columns for Mercury, half a line lower, the figures correspond to the position of Mercury on 3 January, and show it to be in 24° 32′ south declination. Thus, within a span of just three days, the declination of Mercury has decreased by seven minutes (7′). This is an average of just over 2′ per day.

The fact that Mercury is decreasing in declination tells us that between 1 and 3 January Mercury has been moving closer to the celestial equator (dec. 0°). In fact, in Fig. 4 on page 82 you will see that Mercury moves from south declination to north some time between noon on 16 April and noon on 17 April.

In Figs. 1 and 2, the positions for Jupiter, Saturn, Uranus, Neptune and Pluto are given for noon at Greenwich for alternate days. These dates are shown in the first column under the heading 'DM'. Since each of these five planets moves very slowly in declination, it is a simple matter to assess proportionately their positions for dates not shown.

Latitude

Latitude defines the angular distance a planet is north or south of the ecliptic. Neither the Sun nor the Earth can have latitude, for the ecliptic is the Earth's orbit around the Sun. The plane of the ecliptic passes through the centre of both bodies. Astrologers rarely use, or consider, the latitude of a planet when calculating its position relative to the birth chart. While you may safely ignore this co-ordinate when you are beginning to cast charts, you should know that it is used by traditional astrologers in horary and mundane working. This co-ordinate is considered by some to be important when they assess certain aspects made or received by the Moon. In the tables at the bottom of each page in Figs. 1 and 2, the column headed 'Lat', next to the columns for declination, gives the latitude of each planet for alternate dates.

Lunar and
Mutual Aspects

The right-hand side of the top section of Fig. 2 on page 80 lists lunar aspects to the Sun and the planets, and mutual planetary (and solar) aspects for January 2000. It is extremely useful to have these already calculated, in order to see at a glance when particular aspects occur. The actual time of day when an aspect occurs can be found in the section in *Raphael's Ephemeris* entitled A Complete Aspectarian for 2000 (see Fig. 9 on page 85). This section usually covers eight pages, in which all aspects, lunar, solar and mutual planetary, are listed in sequence according to the date and time of occurrence. Refer to pages 7–8 for an explanation of the various aspect symbols.

Lunar Aspects

Each aspect refers to the angular distance between the Moon and a planet measured along the ecliptic in celestial longitude. These are termed lunar aspects because they are aspects formed by the Moon.

There are nine columns. Each column refers to the Moon's aspects to a particular planet. The symbol (or glyph) of the planet aspected by the Moon is shown at the top of the respective column. For example, at the top of the first column we see the Sun's symbol (☉); at the top of the second column the symbol for Mercury (☿); the third column refers to the Moon's aspects to Venus (♀); whilst the successive columns list the Moon's aspects to Mars (♂), Jupiter (♃), Saturn (♄), Uranus (♅), Neptune (♆) and Pluto (♇), in that order.

The Aspects Employed (Lunar)

Not every aspect used by astrologers will be found under Lunar Aspects, but you will recognise the following eight aspects:

♂	conjunction	0°
⊻	semi-sextile	30°
∠	semi-square	45°

35

✶	sextile	60°
□	square	90°
△	trine	120°
⚼	sesquiquadrate	135°
☍	opposition	180°

These aspects appear in the following sequence, covering a full cycle between two successive conjunctions:

☌ ⚺ ∠ ✶ □ △ ⚼ ☍ ⚼ △ □ ✶ ∠ ⚺

The synodic month (or period) of the Moon refers to the time-lapse between two consecutive conjunctions with the Sun. The mean synodic period is 29–53 days, and the deviation from the mean can be as much as 13 hours, which is just over half a day.

Fig. 3 on page 81 is the corresponding page for the month of February. You can use it to check the dates when the Moon conjoins the Sun and each of the planets. The lunar cycle with respect to each planet varies in length throughout the year, according to the position of the planet in the ecliptic relative to the Moon and the Earth. The following table lists the length in days of the Moon's conjunction between January and February 2000:

☽–☉	6 January – 5 February	= 30 days
☽–☿	6 January – 6 February	= 31 days
☽–♀	3 January – 2 February	= 30 days
☽–♂	10 January – 8 February	= 28 days
☽–♃	14 January – 11 February	= 28 days
☽–♄	15 January – 12 February	= 28 days
☽–♅	9 January – 5 February	= 27 days
☽–♆	8 January – 4 February	= 27 days
☽–♇	31 January – 27 February	= 27 days

You can see, therefore, that it is possible for the Moon to form the conjunction with the Sun or a planet twice in one month, if the first conjunction occurs near the beginning of the month and the cycle is 31 days or less.

Finding Lunar Aspects, their Dates and Times

So that you will know immediately where to look in *Raphael's Ephemeris* for a particular lunar aspect, we will examine the

Moon–Sun cycle more closely. Begin by looking for the date when the Moon is in conjunction (σ) with the Sun during January. Running your finger down the column headed $\odot$ in the Lunar Aspects section (Fig. 2), you will find that conjunction (σ) occurs on 6 January (the date is given in the first column on the page).

If you want to know the time when $\mathbb{D}$ σ $\odot$ occurs on 21 January, we turn to Fig. 9 on page 87. This page covers the whole of January and the first 13 days of February. Find 6 January in the first column. The Moon forms ten aspects that day, and one of these is $\mathbb{D}$ σ $\odot$, which occurs at 6.14 pm.

Progressed Lunar Aspects
When thinking in terms of the progressed birth chart, the lunar aspects listed for each month of the year can be seen as aspects formed by the progressed Moon to the progressed Sun and planets (as distinct from the progressed Moon to the natal Sun and planets). For a fuller discussion of progressions, see pages 43–4.

Eclipses and Occultations
A solar eclipse occurs when the centres of the Sun, Moon and Earth are in a straight, or nearly straight, line at the time of the New Moon ($\mathbb{D}$ σ $\odot$). In *Raphael's Ephemeris* this is indicated by ⬤. The Moon is then placed between the Sun and the Earth. A lunar eclipse occurs when the centres of the Sun, Moon and Earth are in a straight, or nearly straight, line at the time of the Full Moon ($\mathbb{D}$ σ^o $\odot$), and in *Raphael's Ephemeris* this is indicated by ⬤. Note that a lunar eclipse occurs on 21 January 2000.

When the Moon is in the same degrees of longitude and declination as a planet, the Moon will, for a brief while, 'hide' or 'eclipse' that planet. This is called an occultation by the Moon. In *Raphael's Ephemeris* it is indicated by the normal conjunction symbol being blacked in, as for the solar eclipse (⬤).

Mutual Planetary Aspects
In the bottom right-hand corner of Fig. 2 are the mutual planetary aspects for January 2000. These are referred to as mutual aspects because they are aspects formed between any two of the planets (the Sun, for convenience, being called a planet) except the Moon.

All the aspects listed on pages 7–8 will be found occurring at least once during January 2000 between particular planets. The numerals at the beginning of each line of the Mutual Aspects table refer to the date in the month. We will now find one of each aspect.

First, look for the conjunction, which indicates that two planets are in the same degree of the ecliptic and the orb is nil. This occurs on 9 January: ♀ ☌ ♇. When two planets are exactly 30° apart they are in semi-sextile aspect: 2 January, ☿ ⩒ ♆. An aspect rarely used by astrologers nowadays is the semi-quintile, implying that the distance measured along the ecliptic between two planets is 36°, which is exactly half the measurement of the quintile: 6 January, ☿ ⊥ ♅. Exactly 45° separates two planets when they are in semi-square aspect: 12 January, ☉ ∠ ♂. The sextile aspect indicates a distance between two planets of 60°: 2 January, ♀ ⚹ ♆. The quintile aspect is an angle of 72°: 2 January, ♂ Q ♄. The square aspect is an angle of 90°: 16 January, ☿ ☐ ♃. The trine aspect is an angle of 120°: 22 January ♀ △ ♃. The sesquiquadrate aspect is an angle of 135°: 8 January, ♀ ⬓ ♃. The bi-quintile aspect is an angle of 144°: 13 January, ♀ ± ♄. The quincunx aspect is an angle of 150°: 8 January, ♀ ▽ ♄.

The opposition aspect is an angle of 180° ☍, meaning that the planets involved are in exactly opposite degrees and signs of the zodiac. This aspect occurs several times in January 2000. The parallel aspect does not refer to measurement along the ecliptic, but in terms of declination north or south of the equator. Two planets forming this aspect are in exactly the same degree of declination, whether on the same side or opposite sides of the equator: 3 January, ♂ P ♄.

When a planet forms more than one aspect on the same day, each aspect is separated by a full stop. For instance, on 6 January, Mercury forms aspects with Saturn and Uranus, and we read:

$$\text{☿ △ ♄ . ☿ ⊥ ♅ .}$$

When all aspects on a particular day cannot be listed in one line against the date, one or more is entered on the next line. This does not happen in January, but in Fig. 3 for 28 February you can read:

☿ ⩒ ♀ . ♀ ☐ ♄ . ♀ ⚹ ♇ . ♂ ⩒ ♄ . ♂ △ ♇ .
♃ P ♇ .

Progressed Aspects

The listing of mutual planetary aspects saves the astrologer having to find aspects formed between two progressed planets (but not between progressed and natal), when dealing with the feature of astrology called progressions. This is further discussed on pages 43–4.

Finding the Times of Mutual Aspects

The exact time when an aspect between two planets occurs can be found in the same way as has been explained for finding the times when lunar aspects occur (see page 37), by reference to the section in *Raphael's Ephemeris* entitled A Complete Aspectarian.

The Moon's Quarters

The four principal phases, or quarters, of the Sun–Moon cycle, or lunation, are indicated by the four important aspects formed by the Sun and Moon:

New Moon	($☽ ☌ ☉$)
First Quarter	($☽ □ ☉$)
Full Moon	($☽ ☍ ☉$)
Last Quarter	($☽ □ ☉$)

At the top of the left-hand page for each month (see Fig. 1, page 79) we see the date and time when the New Moon occurs. At the foot of this page is the date and time of the First Quarter. At the top of the right-hand page for every month (see Fig. 2, page 80) is given the date and time when the Full Moon occurs. At the foot of this page is the date and time of the Last Quarter.

The times when these four phases occur are also given in the section in *Raphael's Ephemeris* entitled A Complete Aspectarian (see Fig. 9, page 87). The times of the New Moon and Full Moon can also be found by referring to Fig. 10 on page 88, which lists the distances apart of all conjunctions and oppositions of all the planets in 2000. The first New Moon of the year is on 6 January at 6.14 pm. This is in celestial longitude.

The declination apart is added for astrologers involved in specialised work, and rarely used as an everyday occurrence. The first Full Moon of the year is on 21 January at 4.40 am, and, because the symbol is blacked out, it indicates that this is also a lunar eclipse. On 5 February at 1.03 pm the next New Moon is shown, and, as it is also filled in, this is a solar eclipse. The filled-in symbols for the inter-planetary conjunctions (superior and inferior conjunctions) are explained on pages 47–9.

Finding the Approximate Longitude of the New Moon

The New Moon has always been considered a very important factor by astrologers. To find just how important a particular New Moon might be in one's own life, the longitudinal position of the New Moon can be related to the planets and angles in one's own natal chart for possible aspects. An orb of 2° should be allowed for aspects from the New Moon position ($\math$ ♂ $\odot$) to natal chart factors. The house in which the New Moon falls is also likely to be of significance, indicating the sphere of one's life activities that will be emphasised during the one-month period of the lunation beginning with the New Moon.

Without using a calculator to find the exact position of the Sun–Moon at the New Moon, one can quite simply note the approximate position, within half a degree or less. As an example, we will find the approximate position of the New Moon occurring in January 2000.

At the top of the page in Fig. 1, note that the New Moon occurs on 6 January at 6.14 pm. Run your finger down the page until you come to the 6th. Since the Sun moves only about 1° in longitude per day, whereas the Moon moves 12°–15° per day, you should use the position of this body. By using the Sun's position at noon, your approximate assessment of the position of the New Moon will be more accurate than if you used that of the Moon as given for noon.

Thus, the time of the New Moon is 6.14 pm, or about six hours after noon. Six hours is one-quarter of 24 hours. With this in mind, note that the Sun at noon on 6 January is in 15° 28′ ♑. The Sun travels about 1°, or 60′, in 24 hours. As New Moon occurs after noon, when the Sun has covered one-quarter (6 hours) of 24 hours, all you need to do to find the approximate position of the New Moon is to add one-quarter of 60′ to the Sun's noon position on 6 January. One-quarter of 60′ = 15′, which added to 15° 28′ ♑ tells us that the New Moon occurs in approximately 15° 43′ ♑.

Indeed, you need not even be quite so precise, yet still risk an error of less than half a degree, by simply using the Sun's noon position on the day of the New Moon.

A Complete Aspectarian

Every aspect formed between the Sun, Moon and planets during the year is listed in *Raphael's Ephemeris 2000* in the section entitled A Complete Aspectarian for 2000 (see Fig. 9, page 87). Aspects are listed in correct sequence for each day according to the time of occurrence. Fig. 9 shows page 30 from the 2000 ephemeris, which covers all aspects for January and part of February.

The first column gives the date and day of the week. The second column gives the aspects. Also listed are the stations of the planets. The third column indicates the time of the day an aspect occurs.

The fourth column states whether (in traditional, and rather outmoded, terminology) an aspect should be considered favourable or unfavourable. Capital G denotes good, small g denotes fairly good, capital B denotes bad, small b denotes fairly bad and capital D denotes doubtful.

Consider the traditionally bad or evil aspects as indicative of tension. Refer to these as difficult aspects. In the same way, the traditionally good aspects should be thought of as signifying ease of expression. Refer to these as easy aspects. Page 7 defines each aspect symbol.

As an example of how to read the data given in this section, in Fig. 9 you can see that on Friday 21 January at 4.40 pm the Moon is opposition Sun (☽ ☍ ☉), and is indicated as a difficult aspect by the capital B. The symbol for the opposition aspect is also filled in, denoting an eclipse of the Moon.

Aspects between Progressed Planets

The listing of aspects in correct sequence according to their time of occurrence simplifies the finding of aspects between two progressed planets or between the progressed Moon and a progressed planet, when using the Secondary System of progressions (one ephemeris day being equal to one year of life).

For a general indication of the year of life when aspects between progressed planets occur, one can use the Mutual Aspects and the

Lunar Aspects on the right-hand page for each month (see Figs. 2 and 3, pages 80 and 81). But to find the actual month within that given year when the aspect occurs, one must refer to the time of day corresponding to this phenomenon as given under A Complete Aspectarian (Fig. 9).

Here is an example for a birth at noon GMT on 4 January 2000. What are the secondary directions between progressed planets (not progressed to natal) for the year 2023, around the person's 23rd birthday? As birth was at noon GMT, the positions of the planets on the birthday will correspond to the 4 January noon date. The 23rd year of life will correspond to a date 23 ephemeris days forward: 4 January + 23 days = 27 January. Thus, the noon positions of the planets on 27 January 2000 correspond to their progressed positions on 4 January 2023.

As we conveniently chose noon GMT for the time of birth in this case, and noon corresponds to January, we can quite simply say that aspects between progressed planets that occur before noon on the progressed date (27 January 2000) will occur some time during the last six months of 2022, whilst aspects listed for the hours after noon will occur some time between January and June 2023.

Referring to Fig. 9, you will find the following aspects between progressed bodies, listed against 27 January 2000, are formed around the 23rd year of life, that is 2022–2023 (note that p indicates a progressed planet:

☿ p ♀ ♃ p.
☽ p ♇ ♂ p. ☽ p ☍ ♃ p. ☽ p ∠ ♇ p

But during which months around the 23rd birthday do these aspects occur? As there are 12 months to the year, and 24 hours to the day, then 1 month is equal to 2 hours. Students conversant with progressed calculations will immediately follow the correspondence of progressed months (centring on the 23rd birthday) with the 12 two-hour divisions of the day given below. Beginner students may not fully understand the procedure until they have studied progressions in detail from a reliable textbook, though it is possible that most will grasp the general idea.

0.00 am 27 January 2000 = 4 July 2002
2.00 am 27 January 2000 = 4 August 2002
4.00 am 27 January 2000 = 4 September 2002
6.00 am 27 January 2000 = 4 October 2002
8.00 am 27 January 2000 = 4 November 2002
10.00 am January 27 2000 = 4 December 2022

p ☽ P ♂ p   (10.46 am)
p ☽ ∠ ♇ p   (11.45 am)
p ☽ ☍ ♃ p   (11.59 am)

12.00 pm January 27 2000 = 4 January 2023
2.00 pm January 27 2000 = 4 February 2023
4.00 pm January 27 2000 = 4 March 2023
6.00 pm January 27 2000 = 4 April 2023
8.00 pm January 27 2000 = 4 May 2023
10.00 pm January 27 2000 = 4 June 2023

p ☿ ♀ ♃ p   (10.14 pm)
p ☽ ♇ ♂ p   (11.42 pm)

The times bracketed against the aspects denote when they occur and are taken from the section A Complete Aspectarian for 2000 (Fig. 9). For instance, any aspect occurring between 4.00 and 6.00 am on 27 January 2000 will correspond with particular trends in the life of this person during September 2022. The Moon opposition Jupiter aspect occurs so near to noon that its influence will be felt at the new year change from 2022 to 2023. Because this is also an important aspect, its influence on the person's life may span a period of up to two years, centring on this special holiday time.

13

Distances Apart of All Conjunctions and Oppositions

The section of *Raphael's Ephemeris* reproduced in Fig. 10 on page 88 is extremely helpful to the astrologer who is interested in studying planetary cycles and their commencement with the conjunction aspect. Every conjunction and opposition occurring during the year is listed in this section, with the date and time and the distance apart in terms of declination at the moment of exact aspect. The section, therefore, provides a complete and compact list of all these important aspects, as well as enabling the duration of each cycle (period between two consecutive conjunctions) to be seen quickly.

Reading the Columns

Look at the listing for January 2000 (Fig. 10). There are four columns for each month. The first column gives the date in the month when the aspect occurs. The second column gives the aspect. The third column states the time at Greenwich when the aspect occurs. The fourth column indicates the distance apart of the two planets in degrees and minutes of declination at the actual moment of exact aspect.

For example, at 10.18 am on 21 January 2000, the Moon is in opposition to Neptune ($\mathrm{\mathbb{D}} \, \mathrm{\varrho^o} \, \Psi$). This reading is, of course, for the Greenwich meridian. For other meridians where GMT is not used, the time as given for Greenwich will need to be converted into the standard time of the country concerned. Or, if the local mean solar time of the aspect is desired for the meridian concerned, the necessary calculation will have to be based on the distance in degrees and minutes of terrestrial longitude between the Greenwich meridian and the other meridian. For these calculations, refer to the chapter on Local Time Differences from GMT on page 63.

Distance Apart in Declination

You may wonder why the distance apart in declination of the two planets forming the conjunction or opposition needs to be given. It does not need to be given, but the conjunction and opposition refer to aspects in celestial longitude. Declination refers to the distance of a planet north or south of the celestial equator. When two planets are within 1° 30′ orb of the same degree, whether on opposite sides or the same side of the equator, they are said to be in parallel aspect.

It follows, therefore, that the closer the planets are in terms of declination when they are also forming an exact conjunction or opposition aspect, the more powerful and significant that aspect is likely to be when related to an individual chart.

For instance, referring again to Fig. 10 on page 88, the Moon is in opposition to the Sun (☽ ☍ ☉) on 21 January 2000, when we read that distance apart in declination is then 0° 18′. But when the conjunction (or New Moon, in the case of the Moon–Sun) occurs on 4 May 2000, their distance apart in declination is as wide as 4° 37′.

Occultations

When an occultation of a planet occurs, the usual conjunction symbol (☌) is shown blacked-in (⚫). This can be seen in Fig. 10 for 4 March when there is an occultation of Venus by the Moon (☽ ⚫ ♀) at 1.12 am. When the Moon is in the same degrees of longitude and declination as a planet, the Moon will, for a brief while, hide or eclipse that planet. This is called an occultation by the Moon. In *Raphael's Ephemeris* this is indicated by the conjunction symbol being blacked in, the same as for a solar eclipse (⚫).

The significance of the blacked-in opposition symbol (☍) in respect of the aspect of 21 January, when the Moon is shown as being in opposition to the Sun (☽☍☉), shows that there is also a lunar eclipse. A lunar eclipse occurs when the centres of the Sun, Moon and Earth are in a straight, or nearly straight, line at the time of a Full Moon (☽☍☉). A solar eclipse occurs when the centres of the Sun, Moon and Earth are in a straight, or nearly straight, line at the time of the New Moon (☽⚫☉).

Great Conjunctions

Great conjunctions are those formed between Jupiter, Saturn, Uranus, Neptune and Pluto. Astrologers specialising in mundane astrology calculate a chart for the time of a great conjunction related to the latitude and longitude of the capital city of a state or country. The country most likely to be affected by the conjunction is considered to be the one in whose chart the conjunction falls most close to an angle (i.e. Ascen, Desc, MC, IC).

During 2000 there is only one of these great conjunctions – between Jupiter and Saturn. As can be noted in Fig. 10, this occurs on 28 May at 4.04 pm (for Greenwich). When either or both planets concerned are retrograde, there can be more than one of the conjunctions, as these planets change direction.

Coincidentally, from 19 May until 30 June there are a series of multiple conjunctions from late Aries and all through Taurus. They finalise in Gemini when five, and sometimes six, planets are all within a 20° arc. This phenomenon does not occur very frequently, but when it does it is often heralded with some extraordinary claims as to what may happen, which can be quite entertaining, to say the least.

This period will prove to be an excellent opportunity to put your expertise in reading *Raphael's Ephemeris* to work.

14

The Daily Motions
of the Planets

When we speak of the daily motion of a planet we mean the distance travelled by that planet (as seen from Earth) in a period of 24 mean solar hours from a given noon to the following noon. This distance can be measured with respect to motion along the ecliptic in terms of celestial longitude, or it can be measured with respect to distance north or south of the equator in terms of declination. It could also apply to a planet's motion north or south of the ecliptic in terms of latitude, but this measurement does not usually concern the astrologer.

The section from *Raphael's Ephemeris* entitled Daily Motions of the Planets, which for convenience includes the Sun and Moon, (see Fig. 6 on page 84) provides useful data. It saves the astrologer the trouble of reckoning these planetary distances from one noon to the next. It also indicates interesting variations in the speed or rate with which a planet moves at particular phases in a cycle.

Only the motions of the planets that may need to be used with a calculator (for calculating proportions of the daily motion) are listed in this section. Thus, we find here the daily motion in longitude of the Sun, the Moon, Mercury, Venus and Mars, and also in terms of declination for the Moon.

Fig. 6 covers the first four months of the year, January–April. Each month has seven columns of figures. The first column, headed with a capital D, refers to the days of the month. The second and third columns give the daily motions in longitude of the Sun (☉) and the Moon (☽). The fourth column refers to the Moon's (☽) daily motion in declination. Columns five, six and seven show the daily motions of Mercury (☿), Venus (♀) and Mars (♂). We will refer to this figure as we discuss the daily movements of the planets in this chapter.

The Daily Motion of the Sun (☉)

The daily motion of the Sun in terms of longitude is given in the second column for each month (Fig. 6), in degrees (°), minutes (′) and seconds (″) of arc. Against 1 January, we read 1° 1′ 10″. This means that from noon on 1 January to noon on 2 January, the Sun travels a distance of 1° 1′ 10″ along the ecliptic as viewed from the Earth.

We can confirm this measurement if we turn to Fig. 1 on page 79, which shows the left-hand page for January 2000. In the fourth column the Sun's longitude position for noon at Greenwich for each day of the month is given. If we subtract the Sun's position for 1 January from its position for 2 January, we will find its daily motion for that period of 24 hours.

Sun at noon 2 January	=	♑	11° 23′ 18″
Sun at noon 1 January	=	♑	10° 22′ 08″
Daily motion	=		1° 1′ 10″

The answer is the same as the daily motion already worked out for us on page 26 of *Raphael's Ephemeris* (Fig. 6).

Because we happen to be situated on the planet Earth, we look out at the Sun, Moon, planets and stars, and they all appear to be revolving round us. The Earth, it seems, is the hub of the universe. But we know that in actual fact the Earth, like the other planets, moves round the Sun, which is the central governing force in the solar system. The illusion that the Earth is at the centre of things is caused by the rotation of our planet on its axis.

We can see, therefore, that in Fig. 6 the daily motion of the Sun is actually the daily motion of the Earth. For instance, whilst the Earth rotates once on its axis between noon on 1 January and noon on 2 January, the position of the Sun as seen from the Earth against the background of stars has shifted to the extent of 1° 1′ 10″ of arc measured along the ecliptic.

The daily motion given for the Sun varies gradually throughout the cycle of one year. In the four months shown in Fig. 6 the greatest motion in one day is that given for both 1 and 2 January, 1° 1′ 10″; whilst the lowest daily motion of the Sun is 0° 58′ 15″, which applies to the period between 30 April and 1 May.

The reason for this variance in the motion of the Sun is the varying speed of the Earth as its orbits the Sun. Annually, around the beginning of January, the Earth is at perihelion, its nearest approach to the Sun. At this phase in its orbit, the Earth moves faster than at any other time; hence, it then covers a maximum distance, and we speak of the Sun attaining a maximum daily motion. We have seen this to be 1° 1′ 10″ for 2000. Around the beginning of July annually, the Earth is at aphelion, when it has reached the point in its orbit furthest from the Sun, and its speed is then at its slowest for the year.

In *Raphael's Ephemeris* the Sun's daily motion is then shown to be at its minimum. In Fig. 7 on page 85 you can check that around the beginning of July the Sun's daily motion averages 0° 57′ 14″. If you turn to Fig. 8 on page 86, you can see that on 2 January the Earth (⊕) is at perihelion, and on 4 July it is at aphelion.

The Daily Motion of the Moon (☽)

The third column for January (Fig. 6) lists the Moon's daily motion in longitude in degrees, minutes and seconds of arc. As will be readily seen, the Moon, being the nearest body to our own planet, moves faster, and therefore covers a greater distance, in a period of 24 hours than the Sun or any of the planets.

For instance, between 1 and 2 January 2000, the Moon's motion along the ecliptic is 11° 57′ 26″. You can appreciate that in the case of the Moon, in particular, it is simpler to turn to the Daily Motions of the Planets section of *Raphael's Ephemeris* (Figs. 6 and 7) to find the Moon's daily motion, than working it out from the noon positions given for consecutive days on the monthly pages.

As has been explained with regard to the varying speed of the Earth in its orbit being shown by the variations in the Sun's daily motion during the year, we can trace the variations in the speed of the Moon, as its position relative to the Earth changes. When the Moon is nearest to the Earth, it is in perigee, and its speed reaches a maximum. Conversely, when the Moon is furthest from the Earth, it is in apogee, when its orbital speed is slowest. This follows Kepler's Law of Equal Areas.

As an example, in Fig. 8 we read that for January 2000 the Moon is at perigee on the 19th. Referring to Fig. 6, we see that for the 24-hour period from noon on 18 January, and the 24-hour period from noon on 19 January, the Moon's daily motion reached a maximum for the month of 14° 58′ 49″ and 15° 02′ 11″ respectively.

In Fig. 8 we again read that on 1 February 2000 the Moon is at apogee. We can, therefore, expect to find its daily motion around the 1 February to be less than it was around 18 January (perigee). And so it is, between 31 January and 1 February (noon to noon) the daily motion of the Moon is the lowest for the month, 11° 48′ 13″.

The Moon's Daily Motion in Declination

The fourth column for each month in Fig. 6 contains the daily motion of the Moon in declination. The Moon always moves fastest, and therefore covers the greatest distance, in declination when it is over the equator. In other words, the smaller the Moon's declination, the greater will be its daily motion. On the other hand, it appears to move slowest, and for a brief period remains stationary, when it attains maximum declination. This is its greatest angular distance (north or south) of the equator.

You can confirm this by turning to Fig. 8 and seeing that on 19 January at 10.30 pm (which is after noon), the Moon attains maximum declination north. In Fig. 6 you can see that between noon on 19 January and noon on 20 January, the Moon's motion in declination is a mere 0° 6′. The only other occasion during the same month when the Moon's declination motion is equally small is on 5–6 January. The Moon is then at maximum declination south.

Turning to Fig. 8 again, you can note that during January the Moon twice crosses the equator, around the 13th and 26th. In Fig. 6 we read that around 13 and 26 January the Moon's daily motion in terms of declination is greatest, implying that the Moon is then moving at its fastest as measured in declination.

The Daily Motion of Mercury (☿)

The fifth column for each month lists the daily motion of Mercury in celestial longitude between consecutive noon positions. Measurements are in degrees and minutes, for, when moving at its fastest, Mercury's daily motion can reach over 2°. Apart from the

Moon (which is not of course a planet), Mercury is the fastest-moving among the planets because, being closest to the Sun, its orbit is the smallest.

The greatest daily motion attained by Mercury during the four months shown in Fig. 6 occurs from noon on 27 January until 31 January, a motion of 1° 45′. In Fig. 7, however, you will find that the maximum daily motion of Mercury for 2000 occurs between 9 and 11 May, 2° 11′ for each of the three 24-hour periods.

The Daily Motion of Venus (♀)

The sixth column for each month (Fig. 6) gives the daily motion of Venus in celestial longitude between any two consecutive noon positions. As Venus can travel along the ecliptic a maximum of around 1° 17′ in a period of 24 hours, as viewed from the Earth, the readings in this column are in degrees and minutes of longitude.

You will notice that in the case of Venus for the year 2000, its movement is relatively constant. From 1 to 22 January it travels at 1° 13′ daily. It then increases speed very slightly to 1° 14′, and remains at this pace until 11 September, when it slows down very slightly once again to 1° 13′ per day. Between September and the end of the year, it slows very gradually to 1° 6′ per day.

The Daily Motion of Mars (♂)

The seventh column for each month (Fig. 6) gives the daily motion of Mars in celestial longitude. As Mars can never travel along the ecliptic more than about 48′ in a period of 24 hours, this column's figures refer only to motion in minutes of longitude.

As an example, the reading for Mars on 1 January 2000 is 47′. This means that the daily motion in longitude of Mars from noon on 1 January to noon on 2 January is 47′.

The Daily Motion of the Slower Planets

The daily motions of the slower-moving planets (Jupiter (♃), Saturn (♄), Uranus (♅), Neptune (♆) and Pluto (♇)) are not given in Fig. 6. This is because their immense distances from the Earth cause them to appear to move very slowly, and therefore they cover a relatively small distance in celestial longitude each day.

We speak of these five outermost planets as slower-moving planets. Jupiter may be seen to move only about 12' in one day when moving at its fastest, whilst Pluto, at its fastest, may move no more than 1' 30". With these planets, therefore, it is a simple matter to estimate by proportion their position in the ecliptic at a given time, when their positions for two consecutive noons are known. Some astrologers, when exactness is not required, use the actual noon position of these five planets for the date given.

15

Phenomena

Page 29 from *Raphael's Ephemeris 2000* is reproduced in Fig. 8 on page 86. Here are listed the dates and times when important astrological phenomena occur during the year. If the data given appears to be rather overwhelming to you, you can relax, for you need not be concerned with any of this data whilst learning the basic theories of chart calculation and interpretation. More advanced astrologers, however, find that this annual page provides a variety of interesting factors that can be employed in research programmes, such as the correlation of events with the periods when a planet is at perihelion, the difference in the effects of Venus or Mercury when in an inferior conjunction with the Sun from those when they are in superior conjunction with the Sun, as well as the varying effects of the Moon in apogee and in perigee.

The Moon in Declination

The motion of the Moon in declination can be traced by looking at the times when this satellite of the Earth is on the equator and at maximum declination north or south of the equator. For example at 9.41 pm on 6 January, the Moon attains maximum declination 20° 57' south of the equator. The Moon then begins to ascend in a northwards sweep towards the equator, which it crosses (from south to north) on 13 January at 3.38 pm. Its motion northwards in terms of declination measurement is continued, until perigee is reached at 10.54pm on 19 January. The Moon then begins its southward journey again, this time crossing the equator (from north to south) at 5.57 am on 26 January.

The Moon in Perigee and Apogee

The Moon's apparent orbit of the Earth is not circular, but traces an ellipse. This means that the Moon's distance from the Earth varies from day to day. The Moon is periodically 'nearest' and 'farthest' from the Earth. When it is at its nearest point in its orbit, we say it is at perigee; whilst when it is at its farthest point, it is at apogee.

For example, the Moon is at perigee at 10.54 pm on 19 January (Fig. 8), at apogee at 1.26 am on 1 February; and is again at perigee at 2.40 am on 17 February.

The Earth at Perihelion and Aphelion
The Earth's orbit of the Sun is not circular, but elliptical. Therefore, from day to day the Earth's distance from the Sun varies, and around 3 January each year the Earth reaches its closest point to the Sun. We then say the Earth is at perihelion. From early January until early July the elliptical shape of the Earth's orbit gradually sweeps our planet further away from the Sun, until around 5 July it reaches its greatest distance from the Sun at aphelion.

The Sun's Entry into Cardinal Signs
The commencement of the four seasons in the Northern Hemisphere, with the entry of the Sun into the Cardinal Signs, has been given in *Raphael's Ephemeris* since 1930. There have been slight variations in the actual wording, but for 2000 (Fig. 8) we read:

20 March	7.35 am	☉ enters ♈	Equinox
21 June	1.48 am	☉ enters ♋	Solstice
22 September	5.28 pm	☉ enters ♎	Equinox
21 December	1.37 pm	☉ enters ♑	Solstice

Eclipses
Usually, though not always, dates of total, partial and annular solar eclipses, and total and partial lunar eclipses are given in the Phenomena section of *Raphael's Ephemeris* (Fig. 8). For further information see page 37.

The Planets at Perihelion and Aphelion
Raphael's Ephemeris (Fig. 8) gives the dates and times, as they periodically occur, of the planets' perihelion and aphelion places in their orbits of the Sun. With Mars, for instance, perihelion (closest approach to the Sun) occurs about 43 or 44 days earlier every two years, which is the planet's sidereal period of 687 days. In Fig. 8 we read that on 2 November 2000 Mars is at aphelion. The previous time was 16 December 1998, and before that, 29 January 1997.

Similarly, when Mars is at perihelion (nearest distance to the Sun during its sidereal period), this occurs 43–44 days earlier every two years. The last occasion of this was 25 November 1999, and before that, on 20 February 1996.

In the case of Venus, the period is much shorter, 224–225 days; whilst Mercury takes 88 days between successive perihelion or aphelion points in its orbit.

The Nodes of the Planets

A planet's north node (Ω) is where its path around the Sun crosses the ecliptic (the Earth's path around the Sun) from south to north. The planet's south node ($\mho$) is where its orbit crosses the ecliptic from north to south. The same symbols are used for the Moon's nodes. The period between two consecutive north nodes, or two consecutive south nodes, is equal to the planet's sidereal period.

Referring to Fig. 8, we can see that Mercury is at its south node at 9.28 am on 20 March 2000 ($\mercury$ in $\mho$) and 88 days later, on 16 June at 8.44 am, Mercury is again at its south node. In that period of 88 days Mercury has completely orbited the Sun. On 25 March at 2.16 pm Mars is at is north node ($\mars$ at Ω). Mars' sidereal period is 687 days. The previous occasion when Mars was at Ω was therefore 687 days earlier, 8 May 1998.

Another point of interest, and an alternative method of finding when a planet is at its node (or close to it), is that when a planet is at its node, its latitude is zero, because it is exactly on the ecliptic.

Greatest Elongation East and West

The apparent angular distance of a planet east or west from its centre of motion (the Sun) at any time is called its elongation. All the planets can reach a maximum elongation of 180°, except for Mercury and Venus, whose greatest possible elongations are about 28° and 48° respectively. Only the positions and times of the greatest elongations of Mercury and Venus are given in the Phenomena section of the *Ephemeris* (Fig. 8) and have appeared since 1906.

For example, on 28 March, Mercury is at greatest elongation west of the Sun, an angle of 28°. Greatest elongation west always follows the planet's inferior conjunction with the Sun, whilst greatest elongation east follows superior conjunction.

The Sun, Moon and Planets' Entry into the Signs

The date and time when the Sun and Moon enter each of the zodiacal signs during the year is given in Fig. 11 on page 89. In that table there are three columns of data to each month. The first column contains the dates when the phenomena occur, the second column indicates whether it is the Sun, the Moon or a planet entering a particular sign, and the third column states the time of the occurrence.

For example, we see that on 2 January 2000 the Moon enters the zodiacal sign Sagittarius (☽ ♐), and that this occurs at 9.32 pm.

Ingress Charts

The term ingress refers to the entry of a body into a sign. The most important ingresses are solar, and these are used in the branch of astrology called Mundane Astrology. This branch studies the trends in national, international and political affairs.

For the current year, a chart would be calculated for the moment of the Sun's entry into each of the four Cardinal signs, and would be generally referred to as ingress charts.

Vernal Ingress: ☉ enters ♈
Summer Ingress: ☉ enters ♋
Autumnal Ingress: ☉ enters ♎
Winter Ingress: ☉ enters ♑

The dates and times when the Sun enters the above Cardinal signs are given on page 58, and in the pages of *Raphael's Ephemeris* shown in Figs. 8 (page 86) and 11 (page 89).

Cuspal Births

This accurate information for when the Sun and Moon enter the zodiacal signs has a particular value when you are calculating a chart for a birth that occurred within a few minutes of when you think the Sun, or perhaps the Moon, is changing signs. If you do not know the exact minute when the Sun or Moon enters a sign, you may not be sure whether to place the Sun or Moon into this new sign or not. Calculations may give the position of the Sun or Moon as 0° 0' of the new sign. But with the aid of the exact data supplied by *Raphael's Ephemeris,* you can check the given birth time with the time of the body's entry into the new sign, and then decide whether to use 29° 59' of one sign or 0° 0' of the next sign.

Local Time Differences from Greenwich Mean Time

The world is divided into 24 time zones, and adjustment has to be made for these when calculating a birth chart away from Greenwich Mean Time – that is, for anywhere abroad. This table of standard time zones was established and adopted at the International Time Conference on 1 October 1884. At this gathering it was decided that the Greenwich Meridian was to be used as the prime meridian, or zero point, and that the world was divided into 24 equal divisions of 15° each.

Any location east of the meridian is, therefore, ahead of GMT, and the time difference has to be subtracted from GMT when calculating the chart. Anywhere west of Greenwich is behind GMT, and must, therefore, be added to the birth time when making your calculations. It is essential that you remember to make these adjustments for the difference in clock time and GMT time each time a chart is calculated. If you refer to Fig. 9 on page 87, you will see that, on 2 January 2000 the Moon is square Mars ($\mathbb{D} \square \mathbb{O}^{7}$) at 7.28 pm.

As an example, let us suppose you want to know what is the local mean time and also the standard time in New York when this aspect occurs. First you must find the local mean time, known as local mean solar time. Due to the rotating of the Earth on its axis, the mean Sun appears to travel over a distance of 15° of arc of terrestrial longitude in 1 hour of mean solar time, or an arc of 1° in 4 minutes. New York is 74° west of Greenwich in terms of terrestrial longitude. If you multiply 74 by 4, and call the answer hours and minutes in mean time, you arrive at 4 hours and 56 minutes.

This tells us that the Sun will take 4 hours and 56 minutes to trace an arc between the meridians of Greenwich and New York. This 4 hours 56 minutes can also be known as the longitude equivalent in time. As the Earth rotates from west to east, and the meridian of New York is west of Greenwich, we see that New York local mean time is behind GMT. That is, New York local mean time is behind GMT by as much as 4 hours 56 minutes. So whatever the time is in Greenwich you have to subtract 4 hours 56 minutes to find the local mean time in New York.

Now in this case, ☽ □ ♂ occurs at 7.28 pm. Subtract 4 hours 56 minutes from 7.28 pm to find what is the equivalent local mean time in New York. The answer is that ☽ □ ♂ occurs at New York on 2 January 2000 at 2.32 pm local mean time.

However, the time system used in New York is Eastern Standard Time (EST), which is 5 hours behind GMT. In terms of EST, therefore, ☽ □ ♂ occurs at 2.28 pm in New York.

On page 93 you will find a table (Fig. 15) (not included in *Raphael's Ephemeris*) that sets out the conversion of longitude to time in order to help in these calculations.

Daylight
Saving Time

Daylight Saving Time (originally called Summer Time) was first introduced into the United Kingdom in 1916. Other countries variously adopted the procedure of advancing clocks one hour during their summer months. You may find details of other countries' conventions in other publications. However, take great care to ensure the information is correct before you undertake the construction of a chart for places other than in the British Isles.

Timescales Used in the United Kingdom
from 1880 Onwards

The timescale used for general purposes in the United Kingdom is Greenwich Mean Time (GMT), except during those periods of Summer Time when the clocks are advanced by one or two hours. Prior to 1 October 1916, the standard time for the whole of Ireland was Dublin mean time (GMT minus 25 minutes). However, during the period 21 May 1916 to 1 October 1916, Irish clocks were advanced by one hour on Dublin mean time. Thereafter, time in Ireland was synchronised with that of Great Britain.

Before 1981, the change from GMT to GMT plus 1 hour (and the reversion) occurred at 2 am GMT. (See the dates in Fig. 16 on page 94). The change from GMT to GMT plus 1 hour (and the reversion) in 1981–1992, and all changes from GMT plus 1 hour to GMT plus 2 hours (and the subsequent reversions) occur at 1 am GMT on the dates given in Fig. 16. All changes occur on Sundays, except for the reversion to GMT from 1917 to 1921 inclusive, and the change to GMT plus 2 hours in 1945, which occurred on Mondays.

Care must be taken with dates before 1925, since the astronomical day began at noon on the civil day of the same date. The dates in Fig. 16 refer to the civil calendar.

GMT plus 1 hour was kept continuously from 18 February 1968 to 31 October 1971. In 1968 Summer Time ended at 2 am GMT on 27 October and was immediately followed by British Standard Time, also equal to GMT plus 1 hour. This was the time system in use between 27 October 1968 and 31 October 1971.

From 1972 to 1980 the following rule applied: Summer Time (GMT plus 1 hour) was the period from the day following the third Saturday in March or, if that day was Easter Day, the day following the second Saturday in March to the day following the fourth Saturday in October. The change occurred at 2 am GMT. From 1981 to 1994 the following rule applied: Summer Time (GMT plus 1 hour) was the period from the last Sunday in March to the day following the fourth Saturday in October. The change occurred at 1 am GMT. The dates for Summer Time (GMT plus 1 hour) given in the Summer Time Order 1997 are in agreement with the EU Directive on Summer Time. They operate from the last Sunday in March to the last Sunday in October, and the changes occur at 1 am GMT.

Since 1 January 1972 the Greenwich time signals have been based on an internationally adopted timescale known as Co-ordinated Universal Time (UTC). This scale is derived from International Atomic Time (TAI) by the occasional insertion of a leap second to keep the scale close to Greenwich mean solar time. Such leap seconds were inserted after the sixtieth second of the last minute of 30 June 1972, of 31 December from 1972 to 79 (inclusive) and of 30 June from 1981 to 1983. Such occasions are marked in the BBC broadcasts by the emission of seven (instead of six) time pips. The beginning of the last (lengthened) pip marks the commencement of the first second of the next minute, as usual.

Local Mean Times of Sunrise and Sunset

Since 1938 the local mean times of sunrise and sunset have been given on pages 40–41 in *Raphael's Ephemeris 2000* Figs. 12 (page 90) and 13 (page 91). The times given are for each Sunday throughout the year. Times are given for Northern Hemisphere latitudes 60°, 55′, 50°, 40°, 30°, 20° and 10°, for the equator, 0°, and for Southern Hemisphere latitudes 10°, 20°, 30°, 40° and 50°.

There is a simple formula for finding the times of sunrise and sunset for intermediate latitudes. The formula is given at the foot of page 41 of *Raphael's Ephemeris* (Fig. 13) for sunset.

If you wish to find the time of sunrise in Jamaica, which is latitude 18° N, on Friday 16 June 2000, you must look at the dates in the first column. There you will find that the nearest two Sundays are on 11 June and 18 June. The nearest latitude is 20° N, the times for which are given in the eighth column.

Now find the local mean time (LMT) for Lat 20° N on 18 June. You should find that this is 5 h 21 m. Next, note the LMT on 18 June for the next nearest latitude to 18° N. This is Lat 10° N and the LMT given is 5 h 40 m.

The next step is a simple proportion. In the example at the foot of Fig. 12 we are given:

$$5 \text{ h } 21 \text{ m} + \tfrac{2}{10} \times 19 \text{ m} = 5 \text{ h } 25 \text{ m}$$

This is not really as complicated as it may appear. The $\tfrac{2}{10}$ refers to the difference in degrees of latitude between 20° N and 18° N as a proportion of the difference in degrees of latitude between 20° N and 10° N. The difference between the former is 2° and the latter 10°, which gives the value for 18° N as $\tfrac{2}{10}$.

As latitude decreases (from 20° to 10°) so does the time of sunrise on 18 June occur later, as can be seen by the times given for sunrise at Lat 20° occurring at 5.21 am, and for Lat 10° occurring at 5.40 am. The difference is 19 minutes, which is the 19 m given in the formula.

The formula states that $\frac{2}{10}$ has to be multiplied by 19. This is equal to asking 'What is $\frac{2}{10}$ of 19?' It is simple to find $\frac{2}{10}$ of 19, if you call 19 the round figure 20. $\frac{2}{10}$ of 20 is clearly 4. The formula states that you add this answer (4 m) to the time of sunrise for Lat 20°. Thus 5 h 21 m plus 4 minutes = 5 h 25 m.

Thus, sunrise at Lat 18° N will occur at 5.25 am on 16 June 2000.

You should now be able to follow the example given at the foot of Fig. 13 for finding the time of sunset in Canberra, and calculate the local mean time of sunrise or sunset for any latitude you wish, for any time of the year.

Sunrise Charts

The main value, perhaps, of the prepared lists of sunrise times for astrologers is that you are able to calculate quickly the time of sunrise for a chart where the time of birth is unknown.

For various reasons, you may not wish to speculate on the possible time of birth, and in such a case you may simply set up what is called a flat chart. For this type of chart you enter the 12 signs, beginning with Aries 0° on the first house cusp, Taurus 0° on the second house cusp, and so on. Since the time of birth is not known, the planets are entered in this type of chart according to their noon position given in *Raphael's Ephemeris* for the birth date. It is to be understood that only generalised indications of character may be given through a flat chart.

Many astrologers set up what is called a sunrise chart, in preference to the flat chart. If you do not wish to go to the trouble of calculating the chart to the true sunrise time, use the planets' noon positions on the birth date, but place the Sun exactly on the first house cusp. In this way, the degree and sign occupied by the Sun can be thought of as the Rising Degree or Ascendant. Usually the houses in this type of sunrise chart are of equal 30° length (as with the Equal House System), and systems such as Placidus are not applied.

The true sunrise chart is, however, a chart calculated in the normal way (as when the time of birth is known), using the true time of sunrise for the latitude of the birthplace and for the date of birth, as though it were the actual moment of birth for the individual concerned.

Tables of Houses

It is customary for Tables of Houses (see Fig. 14 on page 92) for the latitudes of London (51° 30′ N), Liverpool (53° 25′ N) and New York (40° 40′ N) to be given in the annual *Raphael's Ephemeris*. If you do not possess tables for other intermediate latitudes, these three latitudes provide tables that can be conveniently used for many thousands of cities located between the mid-latitudes of 39°–55° north or south of the equator.

What are Tables of Houses?

For an interpretation of a planetary pattern for a given moment to be unique for someone who happens to be born at that same instant, the exact positions of the planets, as viewed from the birthplace of the individual, need to be plotted on to a special chart.

Because the Earth we live on is a sphere, it is obvious that if at a given moment a straight line were drawn between town A and the centre of the Moon, and another straight line drawn between town B (which lies a few miles from town A) and the centre of the Moon, the angle of these two lines will differ. Where towns are hundreds, or thousands, of miles apart, the difference between the respective angles will be considerable.

It is the angle from which the planetary pattern at a given moment is seen from a specified place on Earth, when plotted on a chart, that makes that chart pattern (as the astrologer calls the planetary interrelationship when it is reproduced on the chart form) individual and unique to the person born at that given moment and place.

To plot the planetary pattern, the astrologer employs a basic framework and points of reference. A table of houses for a given latitude enables him to plot the planetary pattern for a given moment for any place located on (or near) that latitude. For instance, the tables prepared for the latitude of London (51° 30′ N) can be used for births in Cardiff (51° 30′ N), Essen, Belgium (51° 28′ N), Kursk, Russia (51° 42′ N) or Santa Cruz, Argentina (50° 01′ S).

The name, Tables of Houses, implies the purpose of these tables. The houses of the birth chart, and especially the angles (first to seventh house cusps, and the MC–IC axis) form the basic framework. By reference to the tables appropriate to a given latitude for a place of birth, the astrologer can find which degrees of the ecliptic (at the moment of birth), as viewed from the birthplace, will be intersected by the cusps of the 12 mundane houses and by the circle of the meridian (which gives the MC and IC). Once this framework of angles and houses is plotted on the chart, the positions of the planets can be fixed.

Although the tables for the latitude of London can be used for the four widely separated cities mentioned above, the Ascendant, Midheaven and other house cusps in each case would be different when calculated for exactly the same moment. This is because their respective locations on Earth in terms of terrestrial longitude are widely different.

How to Read the Tables

The Tables of Houses printed in *Raphael's Ephemeris* (Fig. 14) are calculated for the Placidean system of house cusps. We are not concerned here with defining different house systems, but I would point out that these tables can be used by anyone who favours the Equal House system of charting. By this latter system the 12 houses are of equal length (30° each house), and you simply extract the sign and degree given for the Ascendant (first house cusp), and the sign and degree given for the Midheaven (tenth house cusp in these tables).

Fig. 14 is a reproduction of the first of the two pages for the Tables of Houses for London, as it appears in *Raphael's Ephemeris*. The tables are divided into six sections on each page. Each section covers the period taken by one whole sign (of 30°) to culminate at the Midheaven. Each section is subdivided into seven columns.

The first column is headed 'Sidereal Time'. This refers to the local sidereal time at the moment of birth. H, M and S refer to the reading of sidereal time in hours (H), minutes (M) and seconds (S). For example, in the first section we can read 0H 0M 0S; at the top of the second section, we can read 1H 51M 37S; at the top of the third section, sidereal time begins at 3H 51M 15S.

The second column in each section is headed with the numeral 10. This denotes the tenth house cusp by the Placidean system, but it is also the sign and degree on the Midheaven which we can use for Equal House charting. Directly under 10 in the first section you will recognise the symbol for Aries (♈). This means that all the figures in this column, from 0 to 30, refer to the 30° of the sign Aries. Thus, if the local sidereal time for a birth in London were 0H 0M 0S, we would read under the second column that the sign and degree culminating at the Midheaven is ♈ 0°. For the Placidean system, ♈ 0° would also be the sign and degree on the tenth house cusp.

If you look at the column headed '10' in the second section of the tables you will see under it the symbol for Taurus (♉). This means that all the figures from 0 to 30 in this column refer to the 30° of Taurus. If the local sidereal time for a birth in London were 2H 50M 07S, you would find the sign and degree at the Midheaven (and on the Placidean tenth house cusp) to be ♉ 15°. You will note, therefore, that as sidereal time increases, so will the signs change, until in the full cycle of 24 sidereal hours, each of the 12 zodiacal signs will have culminated at the Midheaven.

The third column in each section is headed '11', which refers to the eleventh house cusp according to the Placidean system only. The fourth column is headed '12', which refers to the twelfth house cusp (Placidean system only).

The fifth column, headed 'Ascen', refers to the Ascendant, which is also the first house cusp, for either Placidean or Equal House systems. The Ascendant is also defined as the degree of the ecliptic rising on the eastern horizon of the observer (or birthplace) at a given moment. In the first section (Fig. 14) the symbol for Cancer (♋) is shown directly under the heading 'Ascen'. If, for example, the local sidereal time for a birth in London were 0H 03M 40S, you would find the Ascendant is ♋ 27° 17′.

The sixth column in each section, headed '2', refers to the second house cusp (Placidean system only). The seventh, and last, column, headed '3', refers to the thirrd house cusp (Placidean system only).

A sign of the zodiac is shown at the top of each column in the tables, and the figures in a column refer to the degrees of the respective sign. You must be careful to notice when there is a change of sign in a column, and not to automatically use the sign given at the top of the column.

If the local sidereal time for a birth in London is 10H 49M 53S, you can arrive at these readings for the Placidean house cusps:

Tenth house cusp (MC)	=	♍	11°
Eleventh house cusp	=	♎	11°
Twelfth house cusp	=	♏	4°
First house cusp (Ascen)	=	♏	20° 50′
Second house cusp	=	♐	22°
Third house cusp	=	♒	1°

If you have noticed that one sign (♏) occupies two house cusps, whilst another sign (♑) is missing, this is because the size of the houses (in degrees) can vary considerably with the Placidean system, particularly when calculating charts for the higher latitudes. The missing sign is what is called an intercepted sign. In the above example it (♑) will be intercepted in the second house.

Once you have calculated the sign and degree for the six house cusps it is a simple matter to enter the sign and degree on the house cusps 4, 5, 6, 7, 8 and 9. The fourth house is opposite to the tenth house; therefore the opposite sign to that on the tenth cusp will appear on the fourth cusp. The same rule applies to each of the other houses. The degrees on opposing cusps remain the same, though in opposing signs. Here is how the rest of the houses in this example should line up:

Fourth house cusp	=	♓	11°
Fifth house cusp	=	♈	11°
Sixth house cusp	=	♉	4°
Seventh house cusp	=	♉	20° 50′
Eighth house cusp	=	♊	22°
Ninth house cusp	=	♌	1°

We now have a second intercepted sign (♋), and it must be opposite to the first intercepted sign (♑). When you use the Equal House system of charting, there is no need to bother with intercepted signs, for houses are of equal 30° length. Therefore, whatever degree is on the Ascendant will also appear on each of the other eleven house cusps, though naturally, in each case the sign will be different. By Equal House charting, the Midheaven (MC) will rarely fall exactly on the tenth house cusp.

The exact Ascendant can be calculated, as can the exact MC. In this example, the Ascendant arrived at is perfectly correct for a birth exactly on latitude 51° 30′ N in London, where the local sidereal time is given as exactly 10H 49M 53S. In most cases, however, the local sidereal time at birth is not exactly identical to any figures given in the Tables of Houses.

In that case you either take the nearest sidereal time in the tables, or, if accuracy is required, use a simple formula for calculating the correct degrees and minutes corresponding to the given local sidereal time.

Use a calculator to subtract the previous day's figure from the day in question. First divide this number by 24, and then multiply the result by the difference in the amount of time. Most astrologers work to the nearest whole degree, and that is usually fairly obvious. Use the 30° mark as your arbiter. If the result is under this, reduce it to the nearest whole degree; if it is above 30°, round it up to the next. This will have little or no effect on the result.

Southern Hemisphere Births

The Tables of Houses given in *Raphael's Ephemeris* (Fig. 14) are for given latitudes in the Northern Hemisphere. These same tables can be used for births on, or near to, the corresponding latitude in the Southern Hemisphere, if a simple additional calculation is made. For instance, the tables for the latitude of London (51° 30′ N) can be used for a birth in Santa Cruz, Argentina, the latitude for which is 50° 01′ south.

To find the local sidereal time for a Southern Hemisphere birth, normal calculations are made as if the birth occurred in the corresponding Northern Hemisphere latitude, until the local sidereal time is arrived at. Now add 12 hours to the local sidereal time. If the figures in the hour column exceed 24, subtract 24 hours. The answer is the local sidereal time at birth for the Southern Hemisphere birth. Then refer to the Tables of Houses for the given latitude to find the sign and degree on the Ascendant and

Midheaven corresponding to the local sidereal time at birth. But the signs given (for Northern Hemisphere births) must be reversed for Southern Hemisphere births. For example, if the Ascendant given in the tables is Libra, we must reverse this and use its opposite sign, which is Aries.

Signs of Long and Short Ascension

Astrologers speak of signs of long ascension and signs of short ascension. In the cycle of 24 hours each of the 12 zodiacal signs must rise over the eastern horizon because of the rotation of the Earth on its axis. From this fact we see that the average time taken by the complete 30° of any sign to rise is two hours. This is 12 (signs) divided into 24 (hours), which equals 2 (hours).

Signs of long ascension are those signs which take longer to rise than the average rising of one whole sign. Signs of short ascension are those signs which rise more quickly than the average rising of one whole sign. This particular distinction between the signs does not apply as one nears the equator.

The reason for this variation in the length of time taken by particular signs to rise is due to the ecliptic lying at an oblique angle across the equator. In the mid-latitudes in the Northern Hemisphere, the signs Cancer to Sagittarius are signs of long ascension, whilst Capricorn to Gemini are signs of short ascension. The reverse applies in the Southern Hemisphere.

London, England is located in a mid-latitude (51° 30′) in the Northern Hemisphere. By referring to the Tables of Houses for London (Fig. 14), you can check how the signs of long ascension take longer to rise (in terms of sidereal time) than do the signs of short ascension.

For example, looking at Fig. 14, you can see that Virgo (♍) is a sign of long ascension. It rises at London when sidereal time is about 3H 10M, and sidereal time reads 6H 00M, when the full 30° of this sign have risen above the horizon. In fact, Virgo takes 2 hours 50 minutes of sidereal time to rise, which is 50 minutes above the average 2 hours. Pisces (♓), a sign of short ascension, takes a mere 52 minutes to rise at London.

Calculations

Every time you construct a chart a certain number of calculations need to be made. Before calculators were so readily available, such reckonings were carried out either in the head as mental arithmetic, or on a piece of paper or by using logarithms. As almost everyone has access to a calculator these days, the calculations have been made much easier.

Not everyone has the consideration to be born precisely in accordance with the data printed in an ephemeris, so astrologers are called upon to calculate the precise position of a planet and adjust it to that birth time. The fastest-moving body is the Moon, whose average daily speed is about 13° 10′, though it can be as high as 15° or as slow as 11°. As a very rough guide, the Moon moves at the rate of about 30′ an hour.

In order to calculate the longitude of the Moon at 2.15 pm on 6 January 2000, you need to know two factors: firstly, since the birth is pm, you need to determine the interval from noon to the given time. Secondly, you need to establish what the Moon's daily motion is between noon on 6 January and noon on 7 January.

The given time is 2.15 pm, therefore the interval is 2 hours 15 minutes.

You can find the daily motion by referring to Fig. 6 on page 84. The Moon's longitude against 6 January is given as 12° 38′ 46″. As 46″ exceeds 30″, we will call this one whole minute, and so the reading for noon on 6 January is adjusted to 12° 39′. The Moon's longitude for 7 January is given as 24° 34′. If you deduct 12° 39′ from 24° 34′, you get 11° 55′. Thus, the daily movement for the 24-hour period from noon on 6 January to noon on 7 January is 11° 55′, a shade under one degree every two hours, or the same average 30′ per hour stated earlier.

Remember that this calculation involves hours and minutes – not hundreds and tens. There are 60 minutes to an hour and 60 seconds to a minute. A quick check of Fig. 6 will confirm this, with a precise reading of 11° 55′ 15″ for this 24-hour period.

Next, reduce the time, 2 hours 15 minutes, to minutes, using a calculator:

$2 \times 60 + 15 = 135$ minutes

Reduce the distance travelled by the Moon, that is 11° 55′, to minutes using a calculator:

$11 \times 60 + 55 = 715$ minutes

Divide 715 by 24 to get the actual movement of the Moon in minutes of arc per hour:

$715 \div 24 = 29.791666$ (or 29.8 when rounded up)

Thus, the Moon moves 29.8 minutes per hour. You, however, want to know how many degrees it would have moved in 2 hours and 15 minutes, or 2 hours plus one quarter of an hour (2.25 hours).

$29.8 \times 2.25 = 67.05$ (or 1° 7′ per hour).

Add 1° 7′ to the Moon's noon position of 12° 38′ and, at 2.15 pm on 6 January, the correct position for the Moon is 13° 45′.

This simple formula for working out the position of the faster-moving planets is easy to follow using a calculator. Once you have made a few attempts, it will soon become almost second nature. You should note that few people work to such precision. For the most part, planets are entered with their positions reduced or increased to whole degrees. Equally, as even fewer people are able to provide a precise birth time from which you may work, there is little need to work to such precision.

With slower-moving planets, working to a reasonable estimate of their position is quite permissible. Neptune, for example, may only move 2 minutes of arc per day, so it is acceptable to use the nearest whole degree. To prove the point, you will note in Fig. 2 (see page 80) that, throughout the whole of January 2000, Neptune advances from 3° 12′ Aquarius on 1 January to only 4° 19′ of the Water Carrier on 31 January, a total of only 1° 7′ for the whole month. It would be quite easy, and quite safe, to estimate its position to the nearest whole degree for any day of the month. For all practical purposes, you could use 3° from 1 to 10 January and 4° from 11 to 31 January.

Glossary of Terms

Aphelion: The point of a planet's orbit where it appears to be at the greatest distance from the Sun.

Apogee: In relation to the Earth, the point of a planet's orbit (including that of the Moon) that appears at its greatest distance.

Ascendant (rising sign): The degree of the zodiac that is 'ascending' on the eastern horizon of the subject at any one time; especially used for time/place of birth in natal charts.

Aspects: Angular measurements on the 360° circle between two planets, or a planet and a significant point on the chart (e.g. ascendant, node). Mutual Aspects are those that do not involve the Moon.

Celestial equator: An imaginary circle on the celestial sphere, at 0° declination, being a projection of the plane of the terrestrial equator.

Celestial latitude/longitude: Celestial latitude marks the distance of a planetary body north or south of the ecliptic; celestial longitude refers to the standard measurement (in degrees and minutes) moving west to east through the zodiac.

Celestial sphere: An imaginary great sphere 'containing' all the celestial bodies, with the earth appearing at its exact centre.

Declination: A measurement taken of the angular distance made by a planet north or south of the celestial equator. (Not to be confused with celestial latitude.)

Descendant: The degree of zodiac exactly opposite to the Ascendant, appearing on the western horizon relative to the observer (e.g. ascen: 15° Taurus = desc: 15° Scorpio.

Ecliptic: The Sun's apparent path through the heavens; in reality, the plane of the Earth's orbit around the Sun. It describes a great circle on the celestial sphere.

Equal House: The most commonly used 'space system' for house division: beginning with the rising degree (first house), the ecliptic is divided into equal 30-degree segments.

Equinox: One of the two points in the year when the sun crosses the celestial equator and day and night are equal in length (from the Latin *aequinoctium*, meaning 'equal night').

Imum coeli: The IC; the lower meridian. On a chart, where the ecliptic reaches its lowest point at the subject's meridian of longitude.

Medium coeli: The MC or Midheaven, opposite to the IC. The degree of ecliptic on a chart which is at its highest point, or culminating, at the subject's meridian.

Meridian: A great (verticular) circle passing through the north (zenith) and south (nadir) poles of the celestial sphere, which is a projection of the terrestrial meridian.

Nadir: The point on the celestial sphere exactly below the subject, at right angles to the horizon of the subject.

Nodes: The two axial points in a planet's orbit, moving from north to south latitude (or vice versa) which intersect the ecliptic. Most often used of the Moon on a natal chart.

Obliquity (of the ecliptic): An angle of approximately 23.5° formed between the planes of the celestial equator and the ecliptic.

Occultation: Used of the Moon's combined celestial longitude and declination; when this is the same as another planet, that planet is 'hidden', hence occultation by the Moon.

Parallel: Used of planets close in declination, north or south of the celestial equator.

Perigee: In relation to the Earth, the point in a planet's orbit (including that of the Moon) that appears at its nearest distance.

Perihelion: The point of a planet's orbit that appears to be at the nearest distance to the Sun.

Polarity: The polar opposite of a sign or house, each pair being connected by innate similarities but 'polarised' by marked differences. Thus Aries/Libra; Taurus/Scorpio; Gemini/Sagittarius; etc.

Precession (of equinoxes): The slow retreat of the vernal equinox point along the ecliptic, which 'precedes' its previous yearly position by 50 seconds every year.

Quadruplicity: The division of the 12 signs into sets of four in three 'modes' of operation: Cardinal (Aries, Cancer, Libra, Capricorn); Fixed (Taurus, Leo, Scorpio, Aquarius); Mutable (Gemini, Virgo, Sagittarius, Pisces).

Retrograde: The apparent retrograde or backward motion in a planet's orbit, which is caused by the Earth's orbit around the Sun 'overtaking' the planet in question.

Sidereal time: The time reckoned by the Earth's rotation with respect to the stars, differing from standard clock time by approximately 4 minutes. A key concept in calculation since the *local* sidereal time for the place of birth establishes the subject's ascendant. A sidereal day is 23 hours 56 minutes and 4 seconds, the actual duration of one rotation of the Earth on its axis.

Solstice: The two 'stations' of the Sun during the year when it reaches its furthest north or south declination; the points of entry into Cancer (summer) and Capricorn (winter).

Triplicity: The division of the 12 signs into sets of three in their four elemental types: Fire (Aries, Leo, Sagittarius); Earth (Taurus, Virgo, Capricorn); Air (Gemini, Libra, Aquarius); Water (Cancer, Scorpio, Pisces).

Vernal equinox: The point where the ecliptic intersects the equator at 10° Aries; the actual beginning of spring when the Sun enters Aries around 21 March. Directly opposite the autumnal equinox where the Sun enters Libra around 22 September.

Zenith: The point on the celestial sphere directly above the subject, at right angles to the horizon of the subject.

Zodiac: The belt of sky that extends approximately 8° either side of the ecliptic, divided into the 12 signs. Known as the Tropical Zodiac (from the Greek, *tropikos* meaning 'turning') based on the turn of the Sun at the solstices. To be distinguished from the Sidereal Zodiac, which uses the constellations of the stars.

2					JANUARY	2000						[RAPHAEL'S	

D	D	Sidereal	☉	☉	☽	☽	☽	☽		Midnight	
M	W	Time	Long.	Dec.	Long.	Lat.	Dec.	Node	☽ Long.	☽ Dec.

D	D	H. M. S.	° ′ ″	° ′	° ′ ″	° ′	° ′	° ′	° ′ ″	° ′
1	S	18 41 50	10♑22 8	23 S 2	13♏19 26	5 N10	10 S 54	5 ♌ 3	19♏19 2	12 S 41
2	Su	18 45 47	11 23 18	22 57	25 16 52	4 53	14 20	4 59	1♐13 19	15 50
3	M	18 49 44	12 24 29	22 52	7♐ 8 48	4 23	17 10	4 56	13 3 38	18 20
4	T	18 53 40	13 25 39	22 46	18 58 10	3 42	19 17	4 53	24 52 40	20 2
5	W	18 57 37	14 26 50	22 39	0♑47 27	2 52	20 34	4 50	6♑42 44	20 53

6	Th	19 1 33	15 28 1	22 32	12 38 46	1 54	20 57	4 47	18 35 47	20 47
7	F	19 5 30	16 29 11	22 25	24 34 0	0 N50	20 23	4 44	0≈33 41	19 45
8	S	19 9 26	17 30 22	22 18	6≈35 2	0 S16	18 53	4 40	12 38 19	17 48
9	Su	19 13 23	18 31 32	22 9	18 43 47	1 23	16 31	4 37	24 51 44	15 2
10	M	19 17 19	19 32 42	22 1	1ℋ 2 27	2 26	13 23	4 34	7ℋ16 16	11 34

11	T	19 21 16	20 33 51	21 52	13 33 20	3 24	9 36	4 31	19 54 30	7 31
12	W	19 25 13	21 35 0	21 42	26 19 37	4 12	5 19	4 28	2 Υ49 12	3 S 3
13	Th	19 29 9	22 36 8	21 33	9 Υ23 35	4 49	0 S43	4 25	16 3 4	1 N39
14	F	19 33 6	23 37 15	21 22	22 47 54	5 12	4 N 2	4 21	29 38 17	6 24
15	S	19 37 2	24 38 22	21 12	6 ♉34 20	5 17	8 43	4 18	13 ♉36 4	10 56

16	Su	19 40 59	25 39 28	21 1	20 43 21	5 4	13 3	4 15	27 55 58	14 59
17	M	19 44 55	26 40 34	20 49	5 ♊13 30	4 31	16 44	4 12	12 ♊35 25	18 13
18	T	19 48 52	27 41 38	20 37	20 1 2	3 40	19 25	4 9	27 29 29	20 17
19	W	19 52 48	28 42 42	20 25	4♋59 50	2 33	20 48	4 5	12♋31 3	20 56
20	Th	19 56 45	29♑43 46	20 12	20 2 1	1 S15	20 42	4 2	27 31 39	20 6

21	F	20 0 42	0≈44 48	19 59	4♌58 51	0 N 7	19 8	3 59	12♌22 38	17 51
22	S	20 4 38	1 45 50	19 46	19 42 3	1 28	16 18	3 56	26 56 22	14 30
23	Su	20 8 35	2 46 51	19 32	4♍ 4 57	2 41	12 31	3 53	11♍ 7 18	10 23
24	M	20 12 31	3 47 52	19 18	18 3 10	3 43	8 8	3 50	24 52 23	5 50
25	T	20 16 28	4 48 52	19 4	1♎34 57	4 29	3 N29	3 46	8♎11 1	1 N 9

26	W	20 20 24	5 49 52	18 49	14 40 50	5 1	1 S10	3 43	21 4 46	3 S 26
27	Th	20 24 21	6 50 50	18 34	27 23 14	5 16	5 37	3 40	3♏36 43	7 44
28	F	20 28 17	7 51 49	18 18	9♏45 47	5 16	9 44	3 37	15 50 59	11 37
29	S	20 32 14	8 52 47	18 2	21 52 53	5 2	13 22	3 34	27 52 6	14 58
30	Su	20 36 11	9 53 44	17 46	3♐49 12	4 35	16 24	3 31	9♐44 45	17 40
31	M	20 40 7	10≈54 40	17 S30	15♐39 19	3 N57	18 S45	3 ♌27	21♐33 24	19 S 37

D	Mercury			Venus			Mars			Jupiter	
M	Lat.	Dec.		Lat.	Dec.		Lat.	Dec.		Lat.	Dec.

	° ′	° ′	° ′	° ′	° ′	° ′	° ′	° ′	° ′	° ′	° ′
1	1 S 0	24 S25	24 S 29	2 N 4	18 S 27	18 S 43	1 S 4	13 S 11	12 S 54	1 S 16	8 N 36
3	1 11	24 32	24 33	2 0	18 58	19 13	1 3	12 37	12 20	1 15	8 38
5	1 21	24 33	24 31	1 57	19 28	19 42	1 1	12 3	11 45	1 14	8 41
7	1 31	24 28	24 24	1 53	19 55	20 8	1 0	11 28	11 10	1 14	8 44
9	1 40	24 18	24 11	1 48	20 21	20 32	0 58	10 53	10 35	1 13	8 47
11	1 47	24 2	23 52	1 44	20 44	20 54	0 56	10 17	9 59	1 13	8 51
13	1 54	23 40	23 27	1 39	21 5	21 14	0 55	9 41	9 23	1 12	8 55
15	1 59	23 12	22 56	1 34	21 23	21 32	0 53	9 5	8 47	1 11	8 59
17	2 3	22 38	22 19	1 29	21 40	21 47	0 52	8 29	8 11	1 11	9 3
19	2 5	21 58	21 36	1 23	21 53	21 59	0 50	7 52	7 34	1 10	9 8
21	2 6	21 12	20 47	1 18	22 5	22 9	0 49	7 15	6 57	1 10	9 13
23	2 5	20 20	19 51	1 12	22 13	22 17	0 47	6 38	6 19	1 9	9 18
25	2 2	19 21	18 50	1 7	22 20	22 22	0 46	6 1	5 42	1 9	9 23
27	1 57	18 17	17 43	1 1	22 23	22 24	0 44	5 23	5 5	1 8	9 29
29	1 49	17 7	16 S 29	0 55	22 24	22 S 24	0 42	4 46	4 S 27	1 8	9 35
31	1 S 39	15 S 51		0 N 49	22 S 22		0 S 41	4 S 8		1 S 7	9 N 41

FIRST QUARTER-Jan.14, 1h.34m. pm. (23°Υ41′)

79 (Figure 1)

FULL MOON-Jan.21, 4h.40m. am. (0°♌26′)

EPHEMERIS]			JANUARY 2000														3
D	☿	♀	♂	♃	♄	♅	♆	♇	Lunar Aspects								
M	Long.	Long.	Long.	Long.	Long.	Long.	Long.	Long.	☉	☿	♀	♂	♃	♄	♅	♆	♇
	° ′	° ′	° ′	° ′	° ′	° ′	° ′	° ′									
1	1♑53	1♐34	27♒58	25♈15	10♉24	14♒49	3♒12	11♐27	✱	∠				☍	□		⊻
2	3 27	2 47	28 44	25 18	10R 23	14 52	3 14	11 29	∠			□					
3	5 1	3 59	29♒31	25 20	10 22	14 55	3 16	11 31	⊻	⊻	☌		⚼			✱	☌
4	6 35	5 12	0♓17	25 23	10 21	14 58	3 18	11 33							✱	∠	
5	8 10	6 25	1 4	25 27	10 20	15 1	3 20	11 36				✱	△	⚼	∠	⊻	
6	9 44	7 37	1 51	25 30	10 19	15 4	3 22	11 38	☌	☌	⊻	∠		△	⊻		⊻
7	11 20	8 50	2 37	25 33	10 19	15 7	3 25	11 40			∠		□				∠
8	12 55	10 3	3 24	25 37	10 18	15 10	3 27	11 42			✱	⊻		□		☌	✱
9	14 31	11 16	4 10	25 41	10 18	15 14	3 29	11 44	⊻	⊻					☌		
10	16 8	12 29	4 57	25 45	10 17	15 17	3 31	11 46	∠	∠		☌	✱			⊻	
11	17 45	13 42	5 43	25 50	10 17	15 20	3 33	11 47		✱	□		∠	✱	⊻	∠	□
12	19 22	14 55	6 30	25 54	10D 17	15 23	3 36	11 49	✱				⊻	∠	∠		
13	21 0	16 9	7 16	25 59	10 17	15 26	3 38	11 51				⊻		⊻	✱	✱	△
14	22 38	17 22	8 3	26 4	10 18	15 30	3 40	11 53	□	□	△	∠	☌				⚼
15	24 17	18 35	8 49	26 9	10 18	15 33	3 42	11 55			⚼	✱		☌		□	
16	25 57	19 48	9 35	26 14	10 18	15 36	3 45	11 57	△	△			⊻		□		
17	27 36	21 2	10 22	26 19	10 19	15 40	3 47	11 59	⚼			□	∠	⊻		△	☍
18	29♑17	22 15	11 8	26 25	10 20	15 43	3 49	12 0		⚼	☍		✱	∠	△	⚼	
19	0♒57	23 28	11 55	26 31	10 20	15 46	3 52	12 2				△		✱	⚼		
20	2 39	24 42	12 41	26 37	10 21	15 50	3 54	12 4					□				⚼
21	4 21	25 55	13 27	26 43	10 22	15 53	3 56	12 6	☍	☍	⚼	⚼		□		☍	△
22	6 3	27 9	14 14	26 49	10 23	15 57	3 58	12 7					△		☍		
23	7 46	28 22	15 0	26 56	10 25	16 0	4 1	12 9			△			△			
24	9 29	29♐36	15 46	27 2	10 26	16 3	4 3	12 11	⚼			☍	⚼			⚼	□
25	11 13	0♑49	16 32	27 9	10 27	16 7	4 5	12 12	△	⚼	□			⚼	⚼	△	
26	12 57	2 3	17 19	27 16	10 29	16 10	4 7	12 14		△					△		✱
27	14 41	3 17	18 5	27 23	10 30	16 14	4 10	12 15				⚼	☍				∠
28	16 26	4 30	18 51	27 30	10 32	16 17	4 12	12 17	□		✱			☍		□	⊻
29	18 11	5 44	19 37	27 38	10 34	16 21	4 14	12 18		□	∠	△			□		
30	19 56	6 58	20 23	27 45	10 36	16 24	4 17	12 20			⊻					✱	
31	21♒41	8♑12	21♓9	27♈53	10♉38	16♒28	4♒19	12♐21	✱			□	⚼		✱	∠	☌

D	Saturn		Uranus		Neptune		Pluto	
M	Lat.	Dec.	Lat.	Dec.	Lat.	Dec.	Lat.	Dec.
	° ′	° ′	° ′	° ′	° ′	° ′	° ′	° ′
1	2S27	12N37	0S39	17S 1	0N14	19S13	10N51	11S24
3	2 26	12 37	0 39	16 59	0 14	19 12	10 52	11 24
5	2 26	12 37	0 39	16 58	0 14	19 11	10 52	11 24
7	2 25	12 37	0 39	16 56	0 14	19 10	10 52	11 25
9	2 24	12 37	0 39	16 54	0 14	19 9	10 52	11 25
11	2 24	12 38	0 39	16 52	0 14	19 8	10 52	11 25
13	2 23	12 38	0 39	16 50	0 14	19 7	10 53	11 25
15	2 23	12 39	0 39	16 48	0 14	19 6	10 53	11 25
17	2 22	12 40	0 39	16 46	0 14	19 5	10 53	11 26
19	2 21	12 41	0 39	16 44	0 14	19 4	10 54	11 26
21	2 21	12 42	0 39	16 42	0 14	19 3	10 54	11 26
23	2 20	12 43	0 39	16 40	0 14	19 2	10 54	11 26
25	2 20	12 45	0 39	16 38	0 14	19 1	10 55	11 26
27	2 19	12 46	0 39	16 36	0 14	19 0	10 55	11 26
29	2 18	12 48	0 39	16 34	0 14	18 58	10 56	11 26
31	2S18	12N50	0S39	16S32	0N14	18S57	10N56	11S26

Mutual Aspects

1 ☉△♄. ♀±♃.
2 ☉⊻♇. ☿⊻♆. ♀Q♅. ♀✱♆. ♂Q♄.
3 ♂P♄. 4 ♀P♆.
6 ☉⊻♅. ☿△♄. ☿⊥♅.
7 ☿⊻♇. ♂P♇.
8 ☉⊥♇. ♀⚼♃. ♀∇♄. ♂⊻♆.
9 ☿⊻♅. ♀☌♇.
11 ☿⊥♇.
12 ☉∠♂. ♀✱♅. ♄ Stat.
13 ♀±♄.
14 ☿∠♂. ☉P♀.
15 ☉⊥♀. ♀∠♆. ♂P♃.
16 ☉☌☿. ☿⊥♀. ☿□♃. ♂⊥♆.
17 ☉□♃. ☉∠♇. ☿∠♇. ♂✱♄.
18 ♂∠♃.
19 ♂□♇. ☿P♀.
21 ☿☌♆. ♀⚼♄.
22 ♀△♃. 23 ♀⊥♆.
24 ☉☌♆. ☿⊥♂. ♂⊻♅.
25 ☿□♄. ♀∠♅. ☉P♆.
26 ☿✱♇. ♃⚼♇. ☉P☿. ☿P♆.
27 ☿Q♃.
28 ☿☌♅. ♀⊻♆. ♂∠♆.
30 ☿⊻♂. ☿P♅.
31 ☉□♄.

LAST QUARTER-Jan.28, 7h.57m. am. (7°♏42′)

FULL MOON-Feb.19, 4h.27m. pm. (0°♍20′)

D M	☿ Long.	♀ Long.	♂ Long.	♃ Long.	♄ Long.	♅ Long.	♆ Long.	♇ Long.
	° ′	° ′	° ′	° ′	° ′	° ′	° ′	° ′
1	23♒25	9♑25	21♓56	28♈ 1	10♉40	16♒31	4♒21	12♐23
2	25 9	10 39	22 42	28 9	10 43	16 35	4 23	12 24
3	26 53	11 53	23 28	28 17	10 45	16 38	4 26	12 26
4	28♒35	13 7	24 14	28 25	10 48	16 42	4 28	12 27
5	0♓16	14 21	25 0	28 34	10 50	16 45	4 30	12 28
6	1 56	15 35	25 46	28 42	10 53	16 49	4 32	12 30
7	3 33	16 49	26 32	28 51	10 56	16 52	4 35	12 31
8	5 8	18 3	27 18	29 0	10 59	16 56	4 37	12 32
9	6 40	19 17	28 3	29 9	11 2	16 59	4 39	12 33
10	8 9	20 31	28 49	29 18	11 5	17 3	4 41	12 34
11	9 33	21 44	29♓35	29 27	11 8	17 6	4 43	12 35
12	10 52	22 58	0♈21	29 37	11 11	17 10	4 46	12 37
13	12 5	24 12	1 7	29 46	11 15	17 13	4 48	12 38
14	13 13	25 26	1 52	29♈56	11 18	17 16	4 50	12 39
15	14 13	26 40	2 38	0♉ 6	11 22	17 20	4 52	12 40
16	15 5	27 54	3 24	0 16	11 26	17 23	4 54	12 41
17	15 49	29♑ 8	4 9	0 26	11 29	17 27	4 56	12 42
18	16 24	0♒22	4 55	0 36	11 33	17 30	4 59	12 42
19	16 50	1 36	5 40	0 46	11 37	17 34	5 1	12 43
20	17 5	2 51	6 26	0 57	11 41	17 37	5 3	12 44
21	17 11	4 5	7 11	1 7	11 46	17 41	5 5	12 45
22	17R 6	5 19	7 57	1 18	11 50	17 44	5 7	12 46
23	16 51	6 33	8 42	1 28	11 54	17 47	5 9	12 47
24	16 27	7 47	9 27	1 39	11 59	17 51	5 11	12 47
25	15 53	9 1	10 13	1 50	12 3	17 54	5 13	12 48
26	15 12	10 15	10 58	2 1	12 8	17 57	5 15	12 49
27	14 23	11 29	11 43	2 12	12 12	18 1	5 17	12 49
28	13 29	12 43	12 28	2 23	12 17	18 4	5 19	12 50
29	12♓30	13♒57	13♈13	2♉35	12♉22	18♒ 7	5♒21	12♐50

Lunar Aspects

D M	☉	☿	♀	♂	♃	♄	♅	♆	♇
1	∠	✱			△	⚻	∠		
2	⊻	∠	☌			△		⊻	⊻
3				✱			⊻		
4		⊻			□			☌	∠
5	●		⊻	∠		□	☌		✱
6		☌	∠	⊻	✱				
7					∠	✱		⊻	□
8	⊻		✱	☌	⊻	∠	⊻	∠	
9	∠	⊻				⊻	∠	✱	△
10	✱	∠	□				✱		
11				⊻	☌			□	⚻
12	□	✱	△	∠		☌	□		
13				✱	⊻			△	
14		□	⚻		∠	⊻	△	⚻	☍
15	△			□	✱	∠	⚻		
16	⚻	△				✱			
17		⚻	☍	△	□			☍	⚻
18				⚻		□	☍		△
19	☍				△				
20		☍	⚻		⚻	△			□
21						⚻		⚻	
22			△	☍			⚻	△	✱
23	⚻						△		∠
24	△	⚻	□		☍			□	
25		△				☍	□		⊻
26				⚻				✱	
27	□	□	✱	△	⚻				☌
28			∠			⚻	✱	∠	
29	✱				△		∠	⊻	

D M	Saturn Lat.	Saturn Dec.	Uranus Lat.	Uranus Dec.	Neptune Lat.	Neptune Dec.	Pluto Lat.	Pluto Dec.
	° ′	° ′	° ′	° ′	° ′	° ′	° ′	° ′
1	2S18	12N51	0S39	16S31	0N14	18S57	10N56	11S26
3	2 17	12 53	0 39	16 28	0 14	18 56	10 57	11 25
5	2 16	12 55	0 39	16 26	0 14	18 55	10 57	11 25
7	2 16	12 57	0 39	16 24	0 14	18 54	10 58	11 25
9	2 15	12 59	0 39	16 22	0 14	18 53	10 58	11 25
11	2 15	13 2	0 39	16 20	0 14	18 52	10 59	11 25
13	2 14	13 5	0 39	16 18	0 14	18 51	10 59	11 24
15	2 14	13 7	0 39	16 16	0 14	18 50	11 0	11 24
17	2 13	13 10	0 39	16 14	0 14	18 49	11 0	11 24
19	2 13	13 13	0 39	16 12	0 14	18 48	11 1	11 23
21	2 12	13 16	0 39	16 10	0 14	18 47	11 1	11 23
23	2 12	13 19	0 39	16 8	0 14	18 46	11 2	11 23
25	2 11	13 22	0 39	16 5	0 14	18 45	11 3	11 22
27	2 11	13 26	0 39	16 3	0 14	18 44	11 3	11 22
29	2 10	13 29	0 40	16 1	0 14	18 43	11 4	11 21
31	2S10	13N32	0S40	15S59	0N13	18S42	11N 4	11S21

Mutual Aspects

1 ☉✱♇. ♂⊥♃.
2 ☿Q♇. ♀Q♂. ♀△♄. ♀⊥♅. ♂⊥♅.
3 ☿∠♀. ♀⊻♇.
4 ☿✱♃. ☿Q♄. ☉P♅. ☿P♄.
6 ☉Q♃. ☉☌♅. ♂∠♄. ☿P♇.
7 ♀⊻♅. ♃Q♅.
8 ☿⊻♆. ♀⊥♇. ☿P♃.
11 ♂⊻♃.
12 ☉⊻♀. ☿✱♄. ☿⊥♆.
13 ☿□♇.
14 ☉Q♇. ☉P♄.
15 ♂∠♅.
16 ☿∠♃. ♀∠♇.
17 ☉⊥♂.
18 ☉Q♄. ♀□♃. ♂✱♆.
19 ☿∠♀. ♂⊥♄. ☉P♇.
20 ☉✱♃.
21 ☉P♃. ☿P♂. ☿Stat.
22 ♀☌♆.
24 ☉⊻♆. ☿∠♃. ♀P♆.
25 ☿⊥♀. 27 ♀✱♂.
28 ☿⊻♀. ♀□♄. ♀✱♇. ♂⊻♄. ♂△♇. ♃P♇.
29 ☿⊻♂. ☿✱♄. ☿□♇.

LAST QUARTER-Feb.27, 3h.53m. am. (7°♐51′)

NEW MOON-Apr. 4, 6h.12m. pm. (15°♈16')

8								APRIL	2000				[RAPHAEL'S

D	D	Sidereal	⊙	⊙	☽	☽	☽	☽		Midnight	
M	W	Time	Long.	Dec.	Long.	Lat.	Dec.	Node	☽ Long.	☽ Dec.

		H. M. S.	° ′ ″	° N	° ′ ″	° S	° S	° Ω ′	° ℋ ′ ″	° S ′
1	S	0 40 37	12 ♈ 3 40	4 N46	2 ℋ 0 12	2 S 36	13 S 11	0 Ω 14	8 ℋ 23 41	11 S 16
2	Su	0 44 34	13 2 52	5 9	14 52 35	3 30	9 11	0 10	21 27 0	6 58
3	M	0 48 30	14 2 1	5 32	28 6 56	4 14	4 S 38	0 7	4 ♈ 52 12	2 S 13
4	T	0 52 27	15 1 9	5 55	11 ♈ 42 33	4 45	0 N15	0 4	18 37 35	2 N45
5	W	0 56 23	16 0 15	6 18	25 36 47	5 0	5 14	0 Ω 1	2 ♉ 39 34	7 41

6	Th	1 0 20	16 59 19	6 40	9 ♉ 45 15	4 57	10 2	29 ♋ 58	16 53 9	12 16
7	F	1 4 16	17 58 20	7 3	24 2 34	4 36	14 19	29 54	1 ♊ 12 48	16 11
8	S	1 8 13	18 57 20	7 25	8 ♊ 23 15	3 57	17 51	29 51	15 33 20	19 9
9	Su	1 12 9	19 56 17	7 48	22 42 36	3 3	20 11	29 48	29 50 38	20 54
10	M	1 16 6	20 55 12	8 10	6 ♋ 57 9	1 58	21 17	29 45	14 ♋ 1 56	21 19

11	T	1 20 3	21 54 5	8 32	21 4 51	0 S 47	21 1	29 42	28 5 49	20 23
12	W	1 23 59	22 52 55	8 54	5 Ω 4 47	0 N27	19 26	29 39	12 Ω 1 44	18 12
13	Th	1 27 56	23 51 43	9 16	18 56 39	1 39	16 43	29 35	25 49 30	14 59
14	F	1 31 52	24 50 29	9 37	2 ♍ 40 15	2 44	13 4	29 32	9 ♍ 28 49	10 59
15	S	1 35 49	25 49 12	9 59	16 15 6	3 39	8 47	29 29	22 58 57	6 29

16	Su	1 39 45	26 47 54	10 20	29 40 14	4 21	4 N 7	29 26	6 ♎ 18 45	1 N43
17	M	1 43 42	27 46 33	10 41	12 ♎ 54 17	4 48	0 S40	29 23	19 26 41	3 S 3
18	T	1 47 38	28 45 10	11 2	25 55 44	5 0	5 22	29 20	2 ♏ 21 19	7 36
19	W	1 51 35	29 ♈ 43 45	11 23	8 ♏ 43 19	4 56	9 44	29 16	15 1 41	11 44
20	Th	1 55 32	0 ♉ 42 19	11 43	21 16 26	4 38	13 36	29 13	27 27 37	15 18

21	F	1 59 28	1 40 50	12 3	3 ♐ 35 25	4 7	16 50	29 10	9 ♐ 40 2	18 9
22	S	2 3 25	2 39 20	12 24	15 41 45	3 25	19 16	29 7	21 40 58	20 10
23	Su	2 7 21	3 37 48	12 44	27 38 5	2 35	20 50	29 4	3 ♑ 33 36	21 16
24	M	2 11 18	4 36 15	13 3	9 ♑ 28 2	1 38	21 28	29 0	15 22 0	21 26
25	T	2 15 14	5 34 40	13 23	21 16 7	0 N37	21 9	28 57	27 11 3	20 37

26	W	2 19 11	6 33 3	13 42	3 ♒ 7 27	0 S 26	19 52	28 54	9 ♒ 6 2	18 54
27	Th	2 23 7	7 31 25	14 1	15 7 30	1 28	17 42	28 51	21 12 30	16 18
28	F	2 27 4	8 29 45	14 20	27 21 42	2 28	14 42	28 48	3 ℋ 35 42	12 55
29	S	2 31 1	9 28 3	14 39	9 ℋ 55 5	3 22	10 58	28 45	16 20 18	8 51
30	Su	2 34 57	10 ♉ 26 20	14 N57	22 ℋ 51 43	4 S 7	6 S 37	28 ♋ 41	29 ℋ 29 37	4 S 16

D	Mercury			Venus			Mars			Jupiter		
M	Lat.	Dec.		Lat.	Dec.		Lat.	Dec.		Lat.	Dec.

	°	°	°	°	°	°	° N	° N	° N	° S	° N
1	1 S 55	7 S 50	7 S 29	1 S 27	3 S 55	3 S 27	0 N 5	13 N54	14 N 8	0 S 55	13 N43
3	2 7	7 6	6 42	1 29	2 58	2 29	0 6	14 23	14 38	0 55	13 52
5	2 17	6 16	5 49	1 29	2 0	1 31	0 7	14 52	15 7	0 55	14 1
7	2 24	5 20	4 51	1 30	1 1	0 S 32	0 9	15 21	15 35	0 54	14 9
9	2 30	4 20	3 47	1 30	0 S 3	0 N27	0 10	15 49	16 2	0 54	14 18

11	2 33	3 14	2 40	1 30	0 N56	1 25	0 11	16 16	16 29	0 54	14 27
13	2 34	2 4	1 27	1 30	1 54	2 24	0 13	16 42	16 55	0 54	14 36
15	2 34	0 S49	0 S 10	1 30	2 53	3 22	0 14	17 8	17 21	0 54	14 44
17	2 31	0 N30	1 N 11	1 29	3 51	4 20	0 15	17 34	17 46	0 53	14 53
19	2 26	1 53	2 35	1 28	4 49	5 18	0 16	17 58	18 10	0 53	15 2

21	2 19	3 19	4 4	1 27	5 47	6 16	0 18	18 22	18 34	0 53	15 10
23	2 10	4 49	5 35	1 25	6 44	7 12	0 19	18 45	18 57	0 53	15 19
25	1 59	6 22	7 10	1 24	7 41	8 9	0 20	19 8	19 19	0 53	15 27
27	1 46	7 58	8 46	1 22	8 37	9 4	0 21	19 29	19 40	0 53	15 36
29	1 31	9 35	10 N 24	1 19	9 32	9 N59	0 22	19 51	20 N 1	0 52	15 44
31	1 S 15	11 N14		1 S 17	10 N26		0 N 23	20 N11		0 S 52	15 N53

FIRST QUARTER-Apr.11, 1h.30m. pm. (21°♋58')

82 *(Figure 4)*

12					JUNE	2000				[RAPHAEL'S

D	D	Sidereal	☉	☉	☽	☽	☽	☽	Midnight	
M	W	Time	Long.	Dec.	Long.	Lat.	Dec.	Node	☽ Long.	☽ Dec.

		H. M. S.	° ′ ″	° ′	° ′ ″	° ′	° ′	° ′	° ′ ″	° ′
1	Th	4 41 7	11 ♊ 17 18	22 N 8	27 ♉ 10 14	4 S 23	15 N15	27 ♋ 0	4 ♊ 36 55	17 N 8
2	F	4 45 3	12 14 49	22 16	12 ♊ 6 38	3 32	18 44	26 57	19 38 16	20 2
3	S	4 49 0	13 12 18	22 23	27 10 36	2 26	20 58	26 53	4 ♋ 42 29	21 32
4	Su	4 52 57	14 9 47	22 30	12 ♋ 12 49	1 S 10	21 43	26 50	19 40 37	21 30
5	M	4 56 53	15 7 14	22 36	27 4 59	0 N10	20 55	26 47	4 ♌ 25 13	19 58
6	T	5 0 50	16 4 41	22 43	11 ♌ 40 45	1 29	18 42	26 44	18 51 10	17 9
7	W	5 4 46	17 2 6	22 48	25 56 15	2 40	15 23	26 41	2 ♍ 55 52	13 24
8	Th	5 8 43	17 59 30	22 54	9 ♍ 50 0	3 39	11 16	26 37	16 38 45	9 1
9	F	5 12 39	18 56 52	22 59	23 22 17	4 25	6 41	26 34	0 ♎ 0 49	4 N19
10	S	5 16 36	19 54 14	23 3	6 ♎ 34 37	4 56	1 N55	26 31	13 3 58	0 S 28
11	Su	5 20 32	20 51 35	23 7	19 29 10	5 10	2 S 50	26 28	25 50 29	5 8
12	M	5 24 29	21 48 54	23 11	2 ♏ 8 13	5 10	7 22	26 25	8 ♏ 22 40	9 30
13	T	5 28 26	22 46 13	23 14	14 34 5	4 54	11 31	26 22	20 42 42	13 24
14	W	5 32 22	23 43 31	23 17	26 48 48	4 25	15 8	26 18	2 ♐ 52 34	16 42
15	Th	5 36 19	24 40 48	23 20	8 ♐ 54 15	3 45	18 5	26 15	14 54 5	19 15
16	F	5 40 15	25 38 5	23 22	20 52 15	2 55	20 13	26 12	26 49 1	20 57
17	S	5 44 12	26 35 21	23 24	2 ♑ 44 36	1 58	21 27	26 9	8 ♑ 39 17	21 43
18	Su	5 48 8	27 32 36	23 25	14 33 19	0 N55	21 43	26 6	20 27 2	21 30
19	M	5 52 5	28 29 51	23 26	26 20 45	0 S 9	21 2	26 3	2 ♒ 14 49	20 20
20	T	5 56 1	29 ♊ 27 6	23 26	8 ♒ 9 38	1 14	19 25	25 59	14 5 38	18 16
21	W	5 59 58	0 ♋ 24 20	23 26	20 3 16	2 15	16 56	25 56	26 2 59	15 25
22	Th	6 3 55	1 21 34	23 26	2 ♓ 5 20	3 12	13 43	25 53	8 ♓ 10 48	11 52
23	F	6 7 51	2 18 48	23 25	14 19 57	4 1	9 52	25 50	20 33 19	7 45
24	S	6 11 48	3 16 2	23 24	26 51 26	4 39	5 31	25 47	3 ♈ 14 48	3 S 12
25	Su	6 15 44	4 13 16	23 22	9 ♈ 43 55	5 5	0 S49	25 43	16 19 10	1 N36
26	M	6 19 41	5 10 29	23 20	23 0 54	5 16	4 N 3	25 40	29 49 22	6 30
27	T	6 23 37	6 7 43	23 18	6 ♉ 44 41	5 9	8 54	25 37	13 ♉ 46 50	11 13
28	W	6 27 34	7 4 57	23 15	20 55 38	4 44	13 25	25 34	28 10 42	15 28
29	Th	6 31 30	8 2 11	23 12	5 ♊ 31 32	3 59	17 18	25 31	12 ♊ 57 22	18 52
30	F	6 35 27	8 ♋ 59 25	23 N 8	20 ♊ 27 22	2 S 58	20 N 8	25 ♋ 28	28 ♊ 0 29	21 N 3

D	Mercury		Venus		Mars		Jupiter	
M	Lat.	Dec.	Lat.	Dec.	Lat.	Dec.	Lat.	Dec.

	° ′	° ′ ° ′	° ′	° ′ ° ′	° ′	° ′ ° ′	° ′	° ′
1	2 N 8	25 N31 25 N 25	0 S 17	21 N27 21 N40	0 N 40	23 N42 23 N 46	0 S 51	17 N51
3	2 0	25 18 25 9	0 13	21 53 22 6	0 41	23 49 23 52	0 51	17 58
5	1 49	24 59 24 47	0 8	22 17 22 28	0 42	23 55 23 58	0 51	18 5
7	1 36	24 35 24 21	0 S 3	22 39 22 48	0 42	24 0 24 2	0 50	18 12
9	1 19	24 7 23 52	0 N 1	22 57 23 6	0 43	24 4 24 6	0 50	18 18
11	0 59	23 36 23 20	0 6	23 14 23 21	0 44	24 8 24 9	0 50	18 25
13	0 37	23 3 22 46	0 11	23 27 23 33	0 45	24 10 24 11	0 50	18 31
15	0 N12	22 27 22 10	0 16	23 38 23 42	0 46	24 12 24 13	0 50	18 37
17	0 S16	21 53 21 35	0 20	23 46 23 49	0 47	24 13 24 13	0 50	18 43
19	0 45	21 17 21 0	0 25	23 51 23 53	0 48	24 13 24 13	0 50	18 49
21	1 17	20 43 20 26	0 29	23 53 23 54	0 48	24 12 24 11	0 50	18 55
23	1 49	20 10 19 54	0 34	23 53 23 52	0 49	24 10 24 9	0 50	19 1
25	2 21	19 39 19 25	0 38	23 50 23 47	0 50	24 8 24 6	0 50	19 7
27	2 53	19 11 18 59	0 43	23 44 23 39	0 51	24 5 24 3	0 50	19 12
29	3 24	18 47 18 N 37	0 47	23 35 23 29	0 52	24 1 23 N 58	0 50	19 18
31	3 S 51	18 N27	0 N 51	23 N23	0 N 52	23 N56	0 S 50	19 N23

FIRST QUARTER-June 9, 3h.29m. am. (18°♍37′)

JANUARY — FEBRUARY

D	☉	☽	☽Dec.	☿	♀	♂	D	☉	☽	☽Dec.	☿	♀	♂
1	1 01 10	11 57 26	3 26	1 34	1 13	47	1	1 00 55	11 50 09	0 39	1 44	1 14	46
2	1 01 10	11 51 56	2 50	1 34	1 13	47	2	1 00 54	11 55 22	0 18	1 43	1 14	46
3	1 01 11	11 49 22	2 07	1 34	1 13	47	3	1 00 53	12 03 13	1 15	1 42	1 14	46
4	1 01 11	11 49 17	1 17	1 35	1 13	47	4	1 00 52	12 13 07	2 10	1 41	1 14	46
5	1 01 11	11 51 19	0 23	1 35	1 13	47	5	1 00 51	12 24 29	2 59	1 40	1 14	46
6	1 01 11	11 55 15	0 34	1 35	1 13	47	6	1 00 49	12 36 51	3 41	1 38	1 14	46
7	1 01 10	12 01 01	1 30	1 36	1 13	47	7	1 00 48	12 49 54	4 13	1 35	1 14	46
8	1 01 10	12 08 45	2 22	1 36	1 13	47	8	1 00 47	13 03 23	4 34	1 32	1 14	46
9	1 01 10	12 18 40	3 08	1 37	1 13	47	9	1 00 45	13 17 12	4 44	1 28	1 14	46
10	1 01 09	12 31 03	3 47	1 37	1 13	46	10	1 00 44	13 31 15	4 40	1 24	1 14	46
11	1 01 09	12 46 07	4 17	1 37	1 13	46	11	1 00 42	13 45 24	4 21	1 19	1 14	46
12	1 01 08	13 03 58	4 36	1 38	1 13	46	12	1 00 40	13 59 17	3 47	1 14	1 14	46
13	1 01 08	13 24 19	4 45	1 38	1 13	46	13	1 00 39	14 12 18	2 55	1 07	1 14	46
14	1 01 07	13 46 26	4 41	1 39	1 13	46	14	1 00 37	14 23 30	1 48	1 00	1 14	46
15	1 01 06	14 09 01	4 20	1 39	1 13	46	15	1 00 35	14 31 41	0 27	0 52	1 14	46
16	1 01 05	14 30 09	3 41	1 40	1 13	46	16	1 00 34	14 35 35	0 58	0 44	1 14	46
17	1 01 05	14 47 31	2 41	1 40	1 13	46	17	1 00 32	14 34 03	2 18	0 35	1 14	46
18	1 01 04	14 58 49	1 23	1 41	1 13	46	18	1 00 30	14 26 30	3 24	0 25	1 14	46
19	1 01 03	15 02 11	0 06	1 41	1 13	46	19	1 00 29	14 13 03	4 11	0 16	1 14	45
20	1 01 03	14 56 50	1 34	1 42	1 13	45	20	1 00 27	13 54 39	4 38	0 05	1 14	45
21	1 01 02	14 43 12	2 50	1 42	1 13	46	21	1 00 26	13 32 54	4 47	0 05	1 14	45
22	1 01 01	14 22 53	3 47	1 43	1 14	46	22	1 00 24	13 09 43	4 41	0 15	1 14	45
23	1 01 01	13 58 13	4 23	1 43	1 14	46	23	1 00 23	12 47 07	4 22	0 24	1 14	45
24	1 01 00	13 31 47	4 39	1 44	1 14	46	24	1 00 21	12 26 47	3 54	0 33	1 14	45
25	1 00 59	13 05 53	4 39	1 44	1 14	46	25	1 00 20	12 10 05	3 18	0 41	1 14	45
26	1 00 59	12 42 24	4 28	1 44	1 14	46	26	1 00 18	11 57 52	2 36	0 49	1 14	45
27	1 00 58	12 22 33	4 07	1 45	1 14	46	27	1 00 17	11 50 40	1 48	0 54	1 14	45
28	1 00 58	12 07 06	3 38	1 45	1 14	46	28	1 00 16	11 48 36	0 56	0 59	1 14	45
29	1 00 57	11 56 19	3 02	1 45	1 14	46	29	1 00 14	11 51 30	0 00	1 02	1 14	45
30	1 00 56	11 50 07	2 20	1 45	1 14	46							
31	1 00 56	11 48 13	1 32	1 45	1 14	46							

MARCH — APRIL

D	☉	☽	☽Dec.	☿	♀	♂	D	☉	☽	☽Dec.	☿	♀	♂
1	1 00 12	11 58 58	0 58	1 03	1 14	45	1	0 59 12	12 52 23	4 00	1 10	1 14	44
2	1 00 11	12 10 18	1 54	1 03	1 14	45	2	0 59 10	13 14 20	4 33	1 12	1 14	44
3	1 00 09	12 24 37	2 46	1 01	1 14	45	3	0 59 08	13 35 38	4 53	1 14	1 14	44
4	1 00 07	12 40 48	3 33	0 58	1 14	45	4	0 59 06	13 54 14	4 59	1 16	1 14	44
5	1 00 06	12 57 38	4 10	0 54	1 14	45	5	0 59 04	14 08 28	4 48	1 18	1 14	43
6	1 00 04	13 13 56	4 36	0 49	1 14	45	6	0 59 02	14 17 19	4 18	1 20	1 14	43
7	1 00 02	13 28 38	4 48	0 44	1 14	45	7	0 59 00	14 20 41	3 29	1 22	1 14	43
8	1 00 00	13 41 00	4 48	0 38	1 14	45	8	0 58 57	14 19 21	2 23	1 24	1 14	43
9	0 59 58	13 50 42	4 31	0 31	1 14	45	9	0 58 55	14 14 33	1 06	1 26	1 14	43
10	0 59 55	13 57 57	3 58	0 25	1 14	45	10	0 58 53	14 07 42	0 16	1 27	1 14	43
11	0 59 53	14 03 03	3 08	0 18	1 14	45	11	0 58 50	13 59 56	1 35	1 29	1 14	43
12	0 59 51	14 06 31	2 03	0 12	1 14	45	12	0 58 48	13 51 52	2 44	1 31	1 14	43
13	0 59 49	14 08 42	0 47	0 05	1 14	44	13	0 58 46	13 43 36	3 38	1 32	1 14	43
14	0 59 47	14 09 35	0 34	0 01	1 14	44	14	0 58 43	13 34 51	4 17	1 34	1 14	43
15	0 59 44	14 08 53	1 52	0 07	1 14	44	15	0 58 41	13 25 09	4 40	1 36	1 14	43
16	0 59 42	14 05 53	3 00	0 12	1 14	44	16	0 58 39	13 14 03	4 47	1 37	1 14	43
17	0 59 40	13 59 56	3 53	0 18	1 14	44	17	0 58 37	13 01 27	4 41	1 39	1 14	43
18	0 59 38	13 50 28	4 29	0 23	1 14	44	18	0 58 35	12 47 35	4 22	1 41	1 14	43
19	0 59 36	13 37 25	4 46	0 28	1 14	44	19	0 58 33	12 33 06	3 53	1 42	1 14	43
20	0 59 34	13 21 14	4 48	0 32	1 14	44	20	0 58 32	12 18 59	3 13	1 44	1 14	43
21	0 59 32	13 03 00	4 35	0 36	1 14	44	21	0 58 30	12 06 21	2 27	1 46	1 14	43
22	0 59 30	12 44 07	4 11	0 40	1 14	44	22	0 58 28	11 56 20	1 34	1 47	1 14	43
23	0 59 28	12 26 07	3 37	0 44	1 14	44	23	0 58 27	11 49 57	0 38	1 49	1 14	43
24	0 59 26	12 10 31	2 55	0 48	1 14	44	24	0 58 25	11 48 03	0 20	1 51	1 14	43
25	0 59 24	11 58 32	2 07	0 51	1 14	44	25	0 58 23	11 51 20	1 16	1 52	1 14	42
26	0 59 23	11 51 05	1 14	0 54	1 14	44	26	0 58 22	12 00 02	2 10	1 54	1 14	42
27	0 59 21	11 48 48	0 18	0 57	1 14	44	27	0 58 20	12 14 12	3 00	1 56	1 14	42
28	0 59 19	11 51 57	0 39	1 00	1 14	44	28	0 58 19	12 33 23	3 44	1 57	1 14	42
29	0 59 17	12 00 29	1 35	1 03	1 14	44	29	0 58 17	12 56 38	4 21	1 59	1 14	42
30	0 59 15	12 14 00	2 29	1 05	1 14	44	30	0 58 15	13 22 21	4 48	2 01	1 14	42
31	0 59 14	12 31 43	3 18	1 08	1 14	44							

MAY

D	☉	☽	☽Dec.	☿	♀	♂
	° ′ ″	° ′ ″	° ′	° ′	° ′	′
1	0 58 14	13 48 19	5 02	2 02	1 14	42
2	0 58 12	14 11 55	5 01	2 04	1 14	42
3	0 58 11	14 30 31	4 40	2 05	1 14	42
4	0 58 09	14 42 07	3 57	2 06	1 14	42
5	0 58 07	14 45 48	2 54	2 08	1 14	42
6	0 58 05	14 42 02	1 35	2 09	1 14	42
7	0 58 04	14 32 19	0 08	2 09	1 14	42
8	0 58 02	14 18 44	1 17	2 10	1 14	42
9	0 58 00	14 03 17	2 31	2 11	1 14	42
10	0 57 58	13 47 33	3 29	2 11	1 14	42
11	0 57 56	13 32 28	4 10	2 11	1 14	42
12	0 57 54	13 18 24	4 35	2 10	1 14	42
13	0 57 52	13 05 21	4 45	2 10	1 14	42
14	0 57 51	12 53 01	4 42	2 09	1 14	42
15	0 57 49	12 41 10	4 28	2 07	1 14	42
16	0 57 47	12 29 39	4 03	2 06	1 14	42
17	0 57 46	12 18 33	3 27	2 04	1 14	41
18	0 57 45	12 08 13	2 44	2 02	1 14	41
19	0 57 43	11 59 12	1 53	2 00	1 14	41
20	0 57 42	11 52 12	0 57	1 58	1 14	41
21	0 57 41	11 48 02	0 01	1 55	1 14	41
22	0 57 40	11 47 26	0 58	1 53	1 14	41
23	0 57 39	11 51 07	1 53	1 50	1 14	41
24	0 57 38	11 59 37	2 43	1 47	1 14	41
25	0 57 37	12 13 14	3 27	1 44	1 14	41
26	0 57 36	12 31 55	4 05	1 41	1 14	41
27	0 57 35	12 55 09	4 34	1 38	1 14	41
28	0 57 34	13 21 47	4 54	1 35	1 14	41
29	0 57 33	13 49 56	5 01	1 32	1 14	41
30	0 57 32	14 17 02	4 52	1 29	1 14	41
31	0 57 31	14 40 07	4 22	1 26	1 14	41

JUNE

D	☉	☽	☽Dec.	☿	♀	♂
	° ′ ″	° ′ ″	° ′	° ′	° ′	′
1	0 57 31	14 56 24	3 29	1 23	1 14	41
2	0 57 30	15 03 57	2 14	1 20	1 14	41
3	0 57 29	15 02 14	0 45	1 17	1 14	41
4	0 57 28	14 52 10	0 48	1 13	1 14	41
5	0 57 26	14 35 46	2 13	1 10	1 14	41
6	0 57 25	14 15 31	3 20	1 07	1 14	41
7	0 57 24	13 53 45	4 07	1 03	1 14	41
8	0 57 23	13 32 17	4 35	1 00	1 14	41
9	0 57 22	13 12 20	4 46	0 56	1 14	41
10	0 57 21	12 54 32	4 45	0 53	1 14	40
11	0 57 20	12 39 04	4 32	0 49	1 14	40
12	0 57 19	12 25 51	4 09	0 45	1 14	40
13	0 57 18	12 14 43	3 37	0 41	1 14	40
14	0 57 17	12 05 28	2 56	0 37	1 14	40
15	0 57 17	11 58 00	2 08	0 33	1 14	40
16	0 57 16	11 52 21	1 14	0 29	1 14	40
17	0 57 15	11 48 43	0 17	0 24	1 14	40
18	0 57 15	11 47 25	0 42	0 20	1 14	40
19	0 57 15	11 48 54	1 37	0 15	1 14	40
20	0 57 14	11 53 37	2 28	0 11	1 14	40
21	0 57 14	12 02 04	3 13	0 06	1 14	40
22	0 57 14	12 14 38	3 51	0 02	1 14	40
23	0 57 14	12 31 29	4 21	0 03	1 14	40
24	0 57 14	12 52 28	4 42	0 07	1 14	40
25	0 57 14	13 16 59	4 53	0 12	1 14	40
26	0 57 14	13 43 47	4 50	0 16	1 14	40
27	0 57 14	14 10 56	4 32	0 20	1 14	40
28	0 57 14	14 35 54	3 52	0 24	1 14	40
29	0 57 14	14 55 50	2 50	0 27	1 14	40
30	0 57 14	15 08 14	1 28	0 30	1 14	40

JULY

D	☉	☽	☽Dec.	☿	♀	♂
	° ′ ″	° ′ ″	° ′	° ′	° ′	′
1	0 57 14	15 11 24	0 07	0 33	1 14	40
2	0 57 14	15 05 06	1 41	0 35	1 14	40
3	0 57 13	14 50 24	3 01	0 36	1 14	40
4	0 57 13	14 29 28	3 59	0 37	1 14	40
5	0 57 13	14 04 54	4 36	0 37	1 14	40
6	0 57 13	13 39 14	4 52	0 37	1 14	40
7	0 57 12	13 14 31	4 52	0 36	1 14	40
8	0 57 12	12 52 09	4 40	0 34	1 14	39
9	0 57 12	12 33 00	4 18	0 32	1 14	39
10	0 57 12	12 17 25	3 46	0 29	1 14	39
11	0 57 12	12 05 23	3 07	0 26	1 14	39
12	0 57 12	11 56 44	2 21	0 22	1 14	39
13	0 57 12	11 51 09	1 29	0 18	1 14	39
14	0 57 13	11 48 19	0 32	0 13	1 14	39
15	0 57 13	11 47 58	0 26	0 08	1 14	39
16	0 57 13	11 49 57	1 23	0 03	1 14	39
17	0 57 14	11 54 11	2 16	0 02	1 14	39
18	0 57 14	12 00 46	3 03	0 08	1 14	39
19	0 57 15	12 09 50	3 42	0 14	1 14	39
20	0 57 16	12 21 35	4 12	0 19	1 14	39
21	0 57 16	12 36 12	4 34	0 25	1 14	39
22	0 57 17	12 53 44	4 45	0 31	1 14	39
23	0 57 18	13 13 59	4 45	0 37	1 14	39
24	0 57 19	13 36 23	4 32	0 42	1 14	39
25	0 57 20	13 59 48	4 02	0 48	1 14	39
26	0 57 21	14 22 37	3 12	0 54	1 14	39
27	0 57 22	14 42 42	2 02	0 59	1 14	39
28	0 57 23	14 57 39	0 35	1 05	1 14	39
29	0 57 24	15 05 22	0 59	1 10	1 14	39
30	0 57 25	15 04 24	2 28	1 15	1 14	39
31	0 57 25	14 54 35	3 41	1 20	1 14	39

AUGUST

D	☉	☽	☽Dec.	☿	♀	♂
	° ′ ″	° ′ ″	° ′	° ′	° ′	′
1	0 57 26	14 36 56	4 30	1 25	1 14	39
2	0 57 27	14 13 35	4 57	1 30	1 14	39
3	0 57 27	13 47 09	5 03	1 34	1 14	39
4	0 57 28	13 20 12	4 53	1 38	1 14	39
5	0 57 29	12 54 55	4 31	1 42	1 14	39
6	0 57 30	12 32 50	4 00	1 46	1 14	39
7	0 57 31	12 14 54	3 20	1 49	1 14	39
8	0 57 31	12 01 31	2 34	1 52	1 14	39
9	0 57 32	11 52 40	1 43	1 55	1 14	39
10	0 57 33	11 48 12	0 47	1 57	1 14	39
11	0 57 34	11 47 34	0 12	1 58	1 14	39
12	0 57 35	11 50 16	1 09	2 00	1 14	39
13	0 57 36	11 55 45	2 04	2 01	1 14	39
14	0 57 37	12 03 27	2 54	2 02	1 14	38
15	0 57 39	12 12 53	3 35	2 02	1 14	38
16	0 57 40	12 23 42	4 08	2 02	1 14	38
17	0 57 41	12 35 40	4 31	2 02	1 14	38
18	0 57 43	12 48 41	4 44	2 01	1 14	38
19	0 57 45	13 02 47	4 45	2 01	1 14	38
20	0 57 46	13 18 00	4 33	2 00	1 14	38
21	0 57 48	13 34 15	4 06	1 59	1 14	38
22	0 57 50	13 51 15	3 22	1 58	1 14	38
23	0 57 52	14 08 20	2 21	1 57	1 14	38
24	0 57 53	14 24 22	1 04	1 56	1 14	38
25	0 57 55	14 37 44	0 24	1 55	1 14	38
26	0 57 57	14 46 35	1 52	1 54	1 14	38
27	0 57 58	14 49 09	3 12	1 52	1 14	38
28	0 58 00	14 44 17	4 13	1 51	1 14	38
29	0 58 02	14 31 50	4 52	1 50	1 14	38
30	0 58 03	14 12 47	5 09	1 49	1 14	38
31	0 58 05	13 49 08	5 07	1 47	1 14	38

d	h	m			PHENOMENA, 2000
Jan.					
2	6	29	pm	☿	in Aphelion
3	5	00	am	⊕	in Perihelion
4	0	36	pm	☽	in Apogee
6	9	41	am	☽	Max. Dec.20°S.57′
13	3	38	pm	☽	on Equator
19	10	30	pm	☽	Max. Dec.20°N.57′
19	10	54	pm	☽	in Perigee
21	4	40	am	◗	Total Eclipse
26	5	57	am	☽	on Equator
Feb.					
1	1	26	am	☽	in Apogee
2	4	36	pm	☽	Max. Dec.20°S.56′
5	1	03	pm	●	Partial Eclipse
9	8	59	pm	☽	on Equator
11	2	21	am	☿	in ☊
15	1	00	am	☿	Gt. Elong.18°E.
15	6	07	pm	☿	in Perihelion
16	7	45	am	☽	Max. Dec.20°N.58′
16	5	24	pm	♀	in ☋
17	2	40	am	☽	in Perigee
22	3	25	pm	☽	on Equator
28	8	48	pm	☽	in Apogee
29	11	54	pm	☽	Max. Dec.21°S. 1′
Mar.					
8	2	47	am	☽	on Equator
14	2	01	pm	☽	Max. Dec.21°N. 6′
14	11	47	pm	☽	in Perigee
20	7	35	am	☉	Enters ♈,Equinox
20	9	28	am	☿	in ☋
21	0	36	am	☽	on Equator
22	1	13	pm	♀	in Aphelion
25	2	16	pm	♂	in ☊
27	5	19	pm	☽	in Apogee
28	7	44	am	☽	Max. Dec.21°S.13′
28	9	00	pm	☿	Gt. Elong.28°W.
30	5	44	pm	☿	in Aphelion
Apr.					
4	10	46	am	☽	on Equator
8	9	58	pm	☽	in Perigee
10	7	17	pm	☽	Max. Dec.21°N.21′
17	8	37	am	☽	on Equator
24	0	22	pm	☽	in Apogee
24	3	51	pm	☽	Max. Dec.21°S.29′
May					
1	8	45	pm	☽	on Equator
6	8	58	am	☽	in Perigee
8	2	05	am	☽	Max. Dec.21°N.35′
9	1	36	am	☿	in ☊
13	5	22	pm	☿	in Perihelion
14	3	22	pm	☽	on Equator
21	11	41	pm	☽	Max. Dec.21°S.40′
22	3	49	am	☽	in Apogee
29	7	06	am	☽	on Equator
Jun.					
3	1	12	pm	☽	in Perigee
4	11	23	am	☽	Max. Dec.21°N.43′
8	8	50	pm	♀	in ☊
9	1	00	pm	☿	Gt. Elong.24°E.
10	9	37	pm	☽	on Equator
16	8	44	am	☿	in ☋
18	6	48	am	☽	Max. Dec.21°S.45′
18	0	43	pm	☽	in Apogee
21	1	48	am	☉	Enters ♋,Solstice
25	4	06	pm	☽	on Equator
26	5	00	pm	☿	in Aphelion

d	h	m			PHENOMENA, 2000
Jul.					
1	7	20	pm	●	Partial Eclipse
1	10	10	pm	☽	in Perigee
1	10	17	pm	☽	Max. Dec.21°N.45′
4	0	00	am	⊕	in Aphelion
8	4	25	am	☽	on Equator
12	8	47	pm	♀	in Perihelion
15	1	09	pm	☽	Max. Dec.21°S.44′
15	3	17	pm	☽	in Apogee
16	1	55	pm	◗	Total Eclipse
22	10	50	pm	☽	on Equator
27	9	00	am	☿	Gt. Elong.20°W.
29	8	57	am	☽	Max. Dec.21°N.45′
30	7	38	am	☽	in Perigee
31	2	25	am	●	Partial Eclipse
Aug.					
4	0	26	pm	☽	on Equator
5	0	52	am	☿	in ☊
9	4	38	pm	☿	in Perihelion
11	7	15	pm	☽	Max. Dec.21°S.45′
11	10	14	pm	☽	in Apogee
19	4	01	am	☽	on Equator
25	5	45	pm	☽	Max. Dec.21°N.49′
27	1	50	pm	☽	in Perigee
31	9	36	pm	☽	on Equator
Sep.					
8	1	48	am	☽	Max. Dec.21°S.53′
8	0	30	pm	☽	in Apogee
12	8	00	am	☿	in ☋
15	9	31	am	☽	on Equator
22	0	11	am	☽	Max. Dec.22°N. 0′
22	4	18	pm	☿	in Aphelion
22	5	28	pm	☉	Enters ♎,Equinox
24	8	13	am	☽	in Perigee
28	7	05	am	☽	on Equator
28	10	12	am	♀	in ☋
Oct.					
5	9	21	am	☽	Max. Dec.22°S. 7′
6	7	01	am	☽	in Apogee
6	10	00	am	☿	Gt. Elong.26°E.
12	5	00	pm	☽	on Equator
19	5	32	am	☽	Max. Dec.22°N.15′
19	10	01	pm	☽	in Perigee
25	3	44	pm	☽	on Equator
Nov.					
1	0	09	am	☿	in ☊
1	5	45	pm	☽	Max. Dec.22°S.23′
2	6	07	am	♀	in Aphelion
2	9	08	pm	♂	in Aphelion
3	3	32	am	☽	in Apogee
5	3	56	pm	☿	in Perihelion
9	2	42	am	☽	on Equator
14	11	10	pm	☽	in Perigee
15	6	00	am	☿	Gt. Elong.19°W.
15	0	09	pm	☽	Max. Dec.22°N.28′
21	10	49	pm	☽	on Equator
29	2	11	am	☽	Max. Dec.22°S.33′
30	11	44	pm	☽	in Apogee
Dec.					
6	1	07	pm	☽	on Equator
9	7	15	am	☿	in ☋
12	9	31	pm	☽	Max. Dec.22°N.34′
12	10	28	pm	☽	in Perigee
19	4	50	am	☽	on Equator
19	3	34	pm	☿	in Aphelion
21	1	37	pm	☉	Enters ♑,Solstice
25	5	22	pm	●	Partial Eclipse
26	9	38	am	☽	Max. Dec.22°S.35′
28	3	16	pm	☽	in Apogee

 (Figure 8)

JANUARY			
1	☽✱☉	5am 34	G
S	♀±♃	5 35	
	☽☍♄	6 10	B
	☽⊻♇	8 16	g
	☉△♄	0pm 37	
	☽□♅	2 59	B
	☽P♇	3 14	D
	☽∠☿	8 12	b
	☽P♄	11 29	B
2	♂Q♄	1am 3	
SU	☽P♂	2 18	B
	☿⊻♆	8 33	
	♀Q♅	1pm 45	
	☽∠☉	2 27	b
	☉⊻♇	2 27	
	☽□♂	7 28	B
	♀✱♆	9 16	
3	☽✱♆	4am 7	G
M	☽☌♀	4 52	G
	☽⊻☿	7 1	g
	☽P♅	10 15	B
	♂P♄	0pm 27	
	☽⚼♃	6 30	b
	☽☌♇	8 54	D
	☽⊻☉	11 41	g
4	☽✱♅	3am 50	G
TU	♀P♆	9 1	
	☽∠♆	10 38	b
	☽P♆	10 38	D
	☽P♀	10 55	G
5	☽⚼♄	0 56	b
W	☽△♃	1 6	G
	☽∠♅	10 25	b
	☽✱♂	0pm 36	G
	☽⊻♆	5 11	g
6	☽⊻♀	0am 41	g
TH	☿⊥♅	1 26	
	☉⊻♅	2 4	
	☽☌☿	5 13	G
	☽△♄	7 18	G
	☽⊻♇	9 56	g
	☽⊻♅	4pm 54	g
	☽☌☉	6 14	D
	☿△♄	8 42	
	☽∠♂	9 3	b
7	☽∠♀	10am 22	b
F	☽□♃	2pm 0	B
	☽∠♇	4 12	b
	♂P♇	4 39	
	☿⊻♇	5 6	
	☽P♀	7 56	G
8	☽⊻♂	5am 13	g
S	☽☌♆	5 44	D
	☽P♆	8 34	D
	♂⊻♆	1pm 46	
	☉⊥♇	4 33	
	♀∇♄	4 51	
	☽□♄	7 22	B
	☽✱♀	7 39	G
	☽✱♇	10 10	G
	♀⚼♃	11 48	
9	☽⊻☿	2am 28	g
SU	☽☌♅	5 4	B
	☽P♅	8 39	B
	☽⊻☉	11 34	g
	♀☌♇	9pm 14	
	☿⊻♅	10 50	
10	☽✱♃	1am 41	G
M	☽∠☿	0pm 12	b
	☽⊻♆	4 48	g
	☽P♄	5 6	B
	☽∠☉	7 22	b
	☽☌♂	8 2	B
11	☽P♇	0am 54	D
TU	☽✱♄	5 47	G
	☽∠♃	6 46	b
	☽P♂	7 31	B
	☽□♇	8 38	B
	☽□♀	0pm 19	B
	☿⊥♇	0 39	
	☽⊻♅	3 23	g
	☽P♃	4 20	G
	☽✱☿	9 5	G
	☽∠♆	9 29	b
12	☽✱☉	2am 23	G
W	☉∠♂	3 8	
	♄ Stat	4 59	
	☽∠♄	10 4	b
	☽⊻♃	11 12	g
	☽∠♅	7pm 33	b
	♀✱♅	9 32	
13	☽✱♆	1am 28	G
TH	☽⊻♂	7 54	g
	☽⊻♄	1pm 38	g
	♀±♄	2 54	
	☽△♇	4 28	G
	☽✱♅	10 57	G
14	☽△♀	1am 23	G
F	☽□☿	11 41	B
	☽∠♂	0pm 27	b
	☽□☉	1 34	B
	☽☌♃	5 47	G
	☽⚼♇	7 12	b
	☉P♀	9 50	
	☿∠♂	11 4	
15	☽⚼♀	6am 21	b
S	☽□♆	7 3	B
	☽P♃	1pm 26	G
	☽P♂	1 52	B
	♀∠♆	2 31	
	☽✱♂	4 4	G
	☽☌♄	6 23	B
	☉⊥♀	6 36	
	♂P♃	7 27	
16	☉☌☿	1am 19	
SU	☽P♇	2 41	D
	☽□♅	3 22	B
	☿⊥♀	4 27	
	☽P♄	9 42	B
	☿□♃	4pm 26	
	♂⊥♆	5 4	
	☽△☉	8 51	G
	☽⊻♃	9 14	g
	☽△☿	9 50	G
17	☿∠♇	2am 47	
M	☉□♃	2 51	
	☽△♆	9 38	G
	♂✱♄	10 28	
	☽P♅	0pm 18	B
	☉∠♇	7 20	
	☽⊻♄	8 19	g
	☽□♂	8 51	B
	☽∠♃	10 0	b
	☽☍♇	11 2	B
	☽⚼☉	11 18	b
18	☽⚼☿	1am 33	b
TU	☽△♅	5 2	G
	☽P♆	8 16	D
	☽⚼♆	10 4	b
	☽☍♀	3pm 55	B
	☽∠♄	8 32	b
	♂∠♃	9 53	
	☽✱♃	10 21	G
19	☽P☉	3am 51	G
W	☽⚼♅	5 14	b
	♂□♇	4pm 6	
	☿P♀	4 23	
	☽✱♄	8 32	G
	☽△♂	11 38	G
20	☽□♃	10 36	B
TH	☽⚼♇	11 17	b
	☽P☉	11 57	G
21	☽⚼♂	0am 55	b
F	♀⚼♄	1 3	
	☽☍☉	4 40	B
	☿☌♆	6 5	
	☽☍♆	10 18	B
	☽☍☿	10 50	B
	☽P♆	0pm 58	D
	☽□♄	8 45	B
	☽⚼♀	10 30	b
	☽△♇	11 34	G
22	♀△♃	4am 58	
S	☽☍♅	5 48	B
	☽P♅	9 13	B
	☽△♃	11pm 53	G
23	☽△♀	1am 30	G
SU	♀⊥♆	4 42	
	☽P♄	10 47	B
	☽P♇	6pm 11	D
	☽△♄	10 48	G
24	☽⚼♃	1am 29	b
M	☽□♇	1 48	B
	☽P♃	5 39	G
	☽☍♂	7 47	B
	☽⚼☉	1pm 24	b
	☽⚼♆	1 45	b
	☉☌♆	6 8	
	☿⊥♂	7 7	
	♂⊻♅	9 42	
	☽P♂	10 8	B
25	☽⚼☿	0am 58	b
TU	☽⚼♄	1 1	b
	☿□♄	1 18	
	☽□♀	10 30	B
	☽⚼♅	11 9	b
	☽△♆	4pm 33	G
	☉P♆	5 6	
	♀∠♅	5 58	
	☽△☉	6 20	G
26	☿✱♇	1am 55	
W	♃⚼♇	3 19	
	☿P♆	4 18	
	☽✱♇	7 27	G
	☽△☿	8 17	G
	☉P☿	1pm 39	
	☽△♅	2 48	G
27	☽P♂	10am 46	B
TH	☽∠♇	11 45	b
	☽☍♃	11 59	B
	☿Q♃	10pm 14	
	☽⚼♂	11 42	b
28	☽✱♀	0am 36	G
F	☽□♆	1 6	B
	♀⊻♆	5 48	
	☽□☉	7 57	B
	☿☌♅	9 55	
	☽P♃	10 43	G
	☽☍♄	1pm 31	B
	☽⊻♇	4 58	g
	☽P♇	10 45	D
	♂∠♆	11 27	
29	☽□♅	0am 56	B
S	☽□☿	3 23	B
	☽△♂	7 11	G
	☽P♄	7 58	B
	☽∠♀	9 27	b
30	☿P♅	9 55	
SU	☽P☿	0pm 36	G
	☽✱♆	0 55	G
	☽P♅	1 12	B
	☽⊻♀	7 6	g
	☿⊻♂	11 18	
	☽P☉	11 39	G
31	☽✱☉	1am 28	G
M	☉□♄	5 15	
	☽☌♇	5 17	D
	☽⚼♃	6 18	b
	☽✱♅	1pm 39	G
	☽P♆	2 40	D
	☽∠♆	7 28	b
	☽□♂	11 58	B
FEBRUARY			
1	☽✱☿	2am 22	G
TU	☽⚼♄	8 21	b
	☽∠☉	10 49	b
	☽△♃	1pm 8	G
	♂⊥♃	3 16	
	☽∠♅	8 17	b
	☉✱♇	11 0	
2	☿Q♇	1am 30	
W	☽⊻♆	2 2	g
	♂⊥♅	8 3	
	♀⊥♅	10 25	
	♀△♄	1pm 7	
	☽∠☿	2 2	b
	♀Q♂	2 2	
	☽△♄	2 52	G
	☽☌♀	3 4	G
	☽⊻♇	6 18	g
	☽⊻☉	8 3	g
3	☽⊻♅	2am 46	g
TH	☿∠♀	0pm 31	
	☽✱♂	4 48	G
	♀⊻♇	10 45	
4	☽∠♇	0am 25	b
F	☽⊻☿	1 10	g
	☽□♃	2 16	B
	☉P♅	2 17	
	☿✱♃	9 31	
	☽☌♆	2pm 22	D
	☿Q♄	3 2	
	☽P♆	6 3	D
	☿P♄	6 10	
5	☽∠♂	0am 32	b
S	☽□♄	2 52	B
	☽✱♇	6 6	G
	☽⊻♀	9 32	g
	☽ • ●	1pm 3	D
	☽☌♅	2 28	B
	☽P♅	6 58	B
	☽P☉	11 23	G
6	☉Q♃	3am 54	
SU	☉☌♅	7 14	
	☽⊻♂	7 38	g
	☽✱♃	1pm 34	G
	♂∠♄	3 59	
	☽∠♀	5 42	b
	☿P♇	6 29	
	☽☌☿	8 52	G
	☽P♄	8 55	B
7	☽⊻♆	0am 43	g
M	☽P♇	6 42	D
	☽P☿	9 35	G
	☽✱♄	0pm 47	G
	♀⊻♅	1 10	
	☽P♃	2 58	G
	☽□♇	3 47	B
	♃Q♅	4 22	
	☽∠♃	6 22	b
8	☽⊻♅	0am 0	g
TU	☽✱♀	1 5	G
	☽⊻☉	3 17	g
	☿⊻♆	3 48	
	☽∠♆	5 3	b
	☿P♃	0pm 38	
	☽∠♄	4 54	b
	☽☌♂	7 46	B
	♀⊥♇	9 42	
	☽⊻♃	10 34	g
9	☽∠♅	3am 54	b
W	☽✱♆	8 48	G
	☽∠☉	9 19	b
	☽⊻☿	0pm 33	g
	☽P♂	2 36	B
	☽⊻♄	8 26	g
	☽△♇	11 11	G
10	☽P♂	2am 32	B
TH	☽✱♅	7 14	G
	☽□♀	1pm 37	B
	☽✱☉	2 39	G
	☽∠☿	6 54	b
11	☽⚼♇	2am 4	b
F	☽⊻♂	5 14	g
	☽☌♃	5 19	G
	♂⊻♃	6 59	
	☽P☿	1pm 17	G
	☽□♆	2 40	B
12	☽✱☿	0am 18	G
S	☽☌♄	1 56	B
	☽P♃	2 29	G
	☽P♇	8 40	D
	☽∠♂	9 2	b
	☿⊥♆	10 0	
	☽□♅	0pm 20	B
	☽P♄	6 23	B
	☿✱♄	6 28	
	☽P☉	10 13	G
	☉⊻♀	11 6	
	☽□☉	11 21	B
	☽△♀	11 22	G
13	☽⊻♃	9am 58	g
SU	☽✱♂	0pm 17	G
	☽P♅	3 47	B
	☽△♆	6 33	G
	☿□♇	11 23	
14	☉Q♇	1am 3	
M	☽⚼♀	3 19	b
	☽⊻♄	5 30	g
	☽☍♇	7 47	B
	☽□☿	8 28	B
	☽∠♃	11 37	b

DISTANCES APART OF ALL ☌s AND ☍s IN 2000

Note: The Distances Apart are in Declination

JANUARY

1	☽☍♄	6am10	2	38
3	☽☌♀	4am52	2	30
3	☽☌♇	8pm54	6	39
6	☽☌☿	5am13	3	35
6	☽☌☉	6pm14	1	37
8	☽☌♆	5am44	0	12
9	☽☌♅	5am04	0	23
9	♀☌♇	9pm14	9	0
10	☽☌♂	8pm02	1	41
14	☽☌♃	5pm47	3	47
15	☽☌♄	6pm23	2	44
16	☉☌☿	1am19	1	58
17	☽☍♇	11pm02	6	41
18	☽☍♀	3pm55	2	4
21	☽•–•☉	4am40	0	18
21	☿☌♆	6am05	2	15
21	☽☍♆	10am18	0	15
21	☽☍☿	10am50	1	59
22	☽☍♅	5am48	0	27
24	☽☍♂	7am47	2	33
24	☉☌♆	6pm08	0	13
27	☽☍♃	11am59	3	52
28	☿☌♅	9am55	1	11
28	☽☍♄	1pm31	2	48
31	☽☌♇	5am17	6	44

FEBRUARY

2	☽☌♀	3pm04	1	21
4	☽☌♆	2pm22	0	17
5	☽•☉	1pm03	1	5
5	☽☌♅	2pm28	0	31
6	☉☌♅	7am14	0	37
6	☽☌☿	8pm52	1	36
8	☽☌♂	7pm46	3	23
11	☽☌♃	5am19	3	55
12	☽☌♄	1am56	2	50
14	☽☍♇	7am47	6	51
17	☽☍♀	0pm51	0	26
17	☽☍♆	10pm21	0	20
18	☽☍♅	7pm05	0	35
19	☽☍☉	4pm27	2	12
20	☽☍☿	8pm59	5	35
22	♀☌♆	8am06	0	29
22	☽☍♂	9am19	3	58
24	☽☍♃	4am59	3	56
25	☽☍♄	0am52	2	50
27	☽☌♇	1pm54	6	59

MARCH

1	☉☌☿	3pm10	3	25
2	☽☌♆	11pm59	0	25
4	♀☌♅	0am39	0	4
4	☽☌♅	1am09	0	39
4	☽•♀	1am12	0	36
5	☽☌☿	1pm19	5	46
6	☽☌☉	5am17	3	14
8	☽☌♂	5pm25	4	26
9	☽☌♃	7pm41	3	55
10	☽☌♄	10am58	2	47
12	☽☍♇	1pm47	7	9
15	☿☌♀	6pm23	2	1
16	☽☍♆	7am36	0	31
17	☽☍♅	6am00	0	45
18	☽☍☿	6am33	2	53
18	☽☍♀	11am24	1	32
20	☽☍☉	4am44	3	57
22	☽☍♂	10am26	4	43
23	☽☍♃	0am45	3	53
23	☽☍♄	2pm47	2	44
25	☽☌♇	10pm16	7	19
30	☽☌♆	9am51	0	38
31	☽☌♅	0pm19	0	53

APRIL

2	☽☌☿	1pm46	1	24
3	☽☌♀	7am44	2	25
4	☽☌☉	6pm12	4	28
6	♂☌♃	6am41	0	59
6	☽☌♃	1pm09	3	50
6	☽☌♂	1pm23	4	50
6	☽☌♄	10pm50	2	40
8	☽☍♇	7pm17	7	29
12	☽☍♆	2pm15	0	46
13	☽☍♅	2pm03	1	1
15	♂☌♄	8pm28	2	10
16	☽☍☿	11pm52	1	54
17	☽☍♀	0pm39	3	4
18	☽☍☉	5pm41	4	41
19	☽☍♃	9pm09	3	47
20	☽☍♄	5am20	2	37
20	☽☍♂	10am36	4	46
22	☽☌♇	5am40	7	36
26	☽☌♆	6pm52	0	55
27	☽☌♅	10pm39	1	10
28	☿☌♀	1pm27	0	17

MAY

3	☽☌♀	9am37	3	33
3	☽☌☿	4pm57	3	50
4	☽☌☉	4am12	4	37
4	☽☌♃	9am05	3	43
4	☽☌♄	1pm27	2	34
5	☽☌♂	8am08	4	31
6	☽☍♇	2am16	7	41
8	☉☌♃	4am08	0	50
8	☿☌♃	6pm53	0	47
9	☉☌☿	3am50	0	1
9	☽☍♆	8pm10	1	2
9	☿☌♄	8pm11	2	3
10	☉☌♄	7pm45	1	56
10	☽☍♅	8pm31	1	17
17	♀☌♃	10am30	0	1
17	☽☍♃	4pm54	3	39
17	☽☍♀	5pm28	3	40
17	☽☍♄	7pm14	2	31
18	☽☍☉	7am34	4	13
18	♀☌♄	0pm56	1	9
19	☽☍☿	9am14	5	12
19	☽☍♂	9am37	4	8
19	☽☌♇	11am40	7	42
19	☿☌♂	0pm26	1	5
19	☿☍♇	11pm41	12	55
20	♂☍♇	8pm25	11	47
24	☽☌♆	2am12	1	8
25	☽☌♅	6am59	1	24
28	♃☌♄	4pm04	1	7

JUNE

1	☽☌♄	5am30	2	29
1	☽☌♃	6am08	3	35
1	☉☍♇	6pm17	11	13
2	☽☌♀	8am01	3	24
2	☽☍♇	11am03	7	40
2	☽☌☉	0pm14	3	30
3	☽☌♂	2am03	3	35
3	♀☍♇	8pm30	11	1
4	☽☌☿	3am36	3	34
6	☽☍♆	3am12	1	11
7	☽☍♅	3am13	1	27
11	☉☌♀	10am31	0	6
14	☽☍♄	7am58	2	27
14	☽☍♃	11am31	3	30
15	☽☌♇	4pm31	7	36
16	☽☍☉	10pm27	2	31
17	☽☍♀	1am50	2	42
17	☽☍♂	7am31	2	55
18	☽☍☿	9pm28	0	6
20	☽☌♆	7am51	1	13
21	☽☌♅	0pm58	1	30
21	♀☌♂	7pm27	0	18
28	☽☌♄	9pm06	2	24
29	☽☌♃	2am34	3	24
29	☽☍♇	8pm33	7	30

JULY

1	☉☌♂	3pm50	0	52
1	☽☌♂	7pm16	2	11
1	☽•☉	7pm20	1	19
2	☽☌♀	4am56	1	37
2	☽☌☿	6am23	3	18
2	☿☌♀	5pm39	4	57
3	☽☍♆	11am55	1	12
4	☽☍♅	11am11	1	29
6	☉☌☿	11am35	4	38
7	☿☌♂	2pm08	5	39
11	☽☍♄	7pm36	2	20
12	☽☍♃	4am52	3	17
12	☽☌♇	9pm09	7	24
15	☽☍☿	9am59	3	16
16	☽☍♂	4am27	1	24
16	☽•–•☉	1pm55	0	2
17	☽☍♀	11am48	0	18
17	☽☌♆	0pm30	1	10
17	♀☍♆	6pm30	1	27
18	☽☌♅	5pm17	1	27
26	☽☌♄	10am20	2	15
26	☽☌♃	8pm35	3	8
27	☽☍♇	5am18	7	18
27	☉☍♆	10pm49	0	12
29	♀☍♅	2am00	0	40
29	☽•☿	5pm19	0	49
30	☽•♂	11am47	0	37
30	☽☍♆	9pm30	1	8
31	☽•☉	2am25	1	12
31	☽☍♅	8pm06	1	24

AUGUST

1	☽•♀	2am14	1	0
8	☽☍♄	6am17	2	8
8	♂☍♆	2pm04	1	15
8	☽☍♃	8pm41	2	58
9	☽☌♇	2am44	7	14
9	☿☍♆	8pm33	1	4
10	☿☌♂	0pm37	0	5
11	☉☍♅	5am20	0	42
13	☽☌♆	5pm16	1	6
14	☽☍♂	0am35	0	9
14	☽☍☿	11am53	0	16
14	☽☌♅	9pm17	1	20
15	☽☍☉	5am13	2	20
16	☿☍♅	6pm43	0	51
16	☽☍♀	7pm58	2	17
22	☉☌☿	1am05	1	39
22	☽☌♄	7pm57	1	59
23	☽☌♃	10am33	2	46
23	☽☍♇	0pm27	7	11
27	☽☍♆	6am25	1	6
28	☽•♂	3am28	0	52
28	☽☍♅	4am44	1	19
29	♂☍♅	7am22	0	24
29	☽☌☉	10am19	3	14
29	☽☌☿	11pm33	2	23
31	☽☌♀	1am21	3	17

SEPTEMBER

4	♃☍♇	10am53	9	48
4	☽☍♄	3pm56	1	52
5	☽☌♇	10am09	7	11
5	☽☍♃	10am17	2	36
9	☽☌♆	11pm05	1	7
11	☽☌♅	2am17	1	19
11	☽☍♂	8pm09	1	31
13	☽☍☉	7pm37	3	58
15	☽☍☿	9am57	4	56
15	☽☍♀	11pm54	4	10
19	☽☌♄	2am01	1	42
19	☽☍♇	6pm30	7	13
19	☽☌♃	7pm40	2	25
23	☽☍♆	1pm34	1	12
24	☽☍♅	11am54	1	21
25	☽☌♂	6pm13	2	5
27	☽☌☉	7pm53	4	25
29	☽☌☿	6pm06	6	42
30	☽☌♀	3am35	4	40

OCTOBER

2	☽☍♄	0am03	1	35
2	☽☌♇	7pm22	7	15
2	☽☍♃	8pm28	2	17
7	☽☌♆	6am17	1	17
8	☽☌♅	8am55	1	26
10	☽☍♂	3pm18	2	35
13	♃☍♇	8am24	9	29
13	☽☍☉	8am53	4	38
15	☽☍☿	4am36	7	29
15	☽☍♀	11pm26	4	47
16	☽☌♄	6am17	1	29
17	☽☌♃	0am42	2	11
17	☽☍♇	1am13	7	18
19	♀☍♄	2am46	3	16
20	☽☍♆	7pm10	1	25
21	☽☍♅	5pm31	1	33
24	☽☌♂	7am59	2	58
27	☽☌☉	7am58	4	33
27	♀☍♃	11am17	2	21
27	☽☌☿	6pm20	5	48
28	♀☌♇	3pm32	11	48
29	☽☍♄	6am04	1	27
30	☉☌☿	2am09	0	38
30	☽☍♃	2am13	2	10
30	☽☌♇	5am32	7	21
30	☽☌♀	9am33	4	23

DISTANCES APART OF ALL ☌s AND ☍s IN 2000 — 39

Note: The Distances Apart are in Declination

NOVEMBER

3	☽ ☌ ♆	2pm36	1	33
4	☽ ☌ ♅	5pm03	1	41
8	☽ ☍ ♂	10am00	3	18
10	☽ ☍ ☿	0pm00	2	36
11	☽ ☍ ☉	9pm15	4	8
12	☽ ☌ ♄	11am12	1	29
13	☽ ☌ ♃	4am03	2	14
13	☽ ☍ ♇	10am22	7	23
14	☽ ☍ ♀	7pm47	3	24
17	☽ ☍ ♆	1am11	1	40
17	☽ ☍ ♅	11pm12	1	49
19	☉ ☍ ♄	0pm42	2	15
21	☽ ☌ ♂	9pm00	3	30
24	☽ ☌ ☿	1pm00	2	39
25	☽ ☍ ♄	9am52	1	33
25	☽ ☌ ☉	11pm11	3	24
26	☽ ☍ ♃	3am50	2	21
26	☽ ☌ ♇	3pm27	7	25
28	☉ ☍ ♃	2am12	0	54
29	☽ ☌ ♀	5pm49	1	59
30	☽ ☌ ♆	11pm22	1	47

DECEMBER

1	☿ ☍ ♄	2pm07	1	21
2	☽ ☌ ♅	2am00	1	56
4	☉ ☌ ♇	2pm03	10	14
7	☿ ☍ ♃	1am10	0	37
7	☽ ☍ ♂	3am50	3	37
9	☽ ☌ ♄	6pm00	1	41
10	☽ ☌ ♃	8am19	2	31
10	☽ ☍ ☿	6pm31	3	8
10	☽ ☍ ♇	10pm13	7	25
11	☽ ☍ ☉	9am03	2	18
12	☿ ☌ ♇	6am11	10	34
12	♀ ☌ ♆	9am24	2	23
14	☽ ☍ ♆	9am51	1	51
14	☽ ☍ ♀	1pm53	0	17
15	☽ ☍ ♅	7am24	2	2
20	☽ ☌ ♂	9am41	3	37
22	☽ ☍ ♄	0pm28	1	47
23	☽ ☍ ♃	3am46	2	41
24	☽ ☌ ♇	0am11	7	27
24	♀ ☌ ♅	5am52	1	10
25	☽ ☌ ☿	5pm15	2	39
25	☽ ● ☉	5pm22	1	2
25	☉ ☌ ☿	7pm23	1	37
28	☽ ☌ ♆	8am00	1	54
29	☽ ☌ ♅	11am09	2	6
29	☽ ☌ ♀	11pm47	1	37

TIME WHEN THE SUN, MOON AND PLANETS ENTER THE ZODIACAL SIGNS IN 2000

JANUARY

2	☽♐	9pm32
4	♂♓	3am01
5	☽♑	10am24
7	☽♒	10pm53
10	☽♓	9am59
12	☽♈	6pm48
15	☽♉	0am38
17	☽♊	3am25
18	☿♒	10pm20
19	☽♋	4am01
20	☉♒	6pm23
21	☽♌	3am58
23	☽♍	5am07
24	♀♑	7pm52
25	☽♎	9am09
27	☽♏	5pm01
30	☽♐	4am17

FEBRUARY

1	☽♑	5pm10
4	☽♒	5am31
5	☿♓	8am09
6	☽♓	4pm02
9	☽♈	0am17
11	☽♉	6am21
12	♂♈	1am04
13	☽♊	10am23
14	♃♉	9pm39
15	☽♋	0pm45
17	☽♌	2pm11
18	♀♒	4am43
19	☉♓	8am33
19	☽♍	3pm53
21	☽♎	7pm21
24	☽♏	1am58
26	☽♐	0pm10
29	☽♑	0am45

MARCH

2	☽♒	1pm14
4	☽♓	11pm30
7	☽♈	6am54
9	☽♉	0pm01
11	☽♊	3pm46
13	♀♓	11am36
13	☽♋	6pm51
15	☽♌	9pm43
18	☽♍	0am48
20	☽♎	4am57
20	☉♈	7am35
22	☽♏	11am17
23	♂♉	1am25
24	☽♐	8pm43
27	☽♑	8am51
29	☽♒	9pm34

APRIL

1	☽♓	8am12
3	☽♈	3pm22
5	☽♉	7pm29
6	♀♈	6pm37
7	☽♊	9pm58
10	☽♋	0am16
12	☽♌	3am16
13	☿♈	0am17
14	☽♍	7am19
16	☽♎	0pm36
18	☽♏	7pm35
19	☉♉	6pm39
21	☽♐	4am58
23	☽♑	4pm47
26	☽♒	5am42
28	☽♓	5pm06
30	☿♉	3am53

MAY

1	☽♈	0am55
1	♀♉	2am49
3	☽♉	4am54
3	♂♊	7pm18
5	☽♊	6am23
7	☽♋	7am14
9	☽♌	9am01
11	☽♍	0pm41
13	☽♎	6pm27
14	☿♊	7am10
16	☽♏	2am16
18	☽♐	0pm09
20	☉♊	5pm49
21	☽♑	0am01
23	☽♒	1pm00
25	♀♊	0pm15
26	☽♓	1am07
28	☽♈	10am08
30	☿♋	4am27
30	☽♉	3pm02

JUNE

1	☽♊	4pm34
3	☽♋	4pm30
5	☽♌	4pm45
7	☽♍	6pm57
9	☽♎	11pm59
12	☽♏	7am55
14	☽♐	6pm18
16	♂♋	0pm30
17	☽♑	6am26
18	♀♋	10pm15
19	☽♒	7pm26
21	☉♋	1am48
22	☽♓	7am52
24	☽♈	5pm55
27	☽♉	0am19
29	☽♊	2am59
30	♃♊	7am34

JULY

1	☽♋	3am09
3	☽♌	2am38
5	☽♍	3am19
7	☽♎	6am47
9	☽♏	1pm48
12	☽♐	0am06
13	♀♌	8am02
14	☽♑	0pm28
17	☽♒	1am27
19	☽♓	1pm44
22	☽♈	0am09
22	☉♌	0pm43
24	☽♉	7am44
26	☽♊	0pm01
28	☽♋	1pm30
30	☽♌	1pm23

AUGUST

1	♂♌	1am21
1	☽♍	1pm27
3	☽♎	3pm31
5	☽♏	9pm04
6	♀♍	5pm32
7	☿♌	5am42
8	☽♐	6am30
10	♄♊	2am25
10	☽♑	6pm44
13	☽♒	7am43
15	☽♓	7pm41
18	☽♈	5am44
20	☽♉	1pm31
22	☿♍	10am11
22	☽♊	6pm55
22	☉♍	7pm49
24	☽♋	10pm00
26	☽♌	11pm17
28	☽♍	11pm55
31	☽♎	1am33
31	♀♎	3am35

SEPTEMBER

2	☽♏	5am55
4	☽♐	2pm08
7	☽♑	1am47
7	☿♎	10pm22
9	☽♒	2pm44
12	☽♓	2am34
14	☽♈	0pm00
16	☽♉	7pm05
17	♂♍	0am19
19	☽♊	0am22
21	☽♋	4am16
22	☉♎	5pm28
23	☽♌	7am00
24	♀♏	3pm26
25	☽♍	9am02
27	☽♎	11am22
28	☿♏	1pm28
29	☽♏	3pm29

OCTOBER

1	☽♐	10pm50
4	☽♑	9am42
6	☽♒	10pm33
9	☽♓	10am36
11	☽♈	7pm51
14	☽♉	2am06
16	♄♉	0am46
16	☽♊	6am19
18	☽♋	9am37
19	♀♐	6am18
20	☽♌	0pm42
22	☽♍	3pm52
23	☉♏	2am47
24	☽♎	7pm30
27	☽♏	0am23
29	☽♐	7am40
31	☽♑	6pm01

NOVEMBER

3	☽♒	6am41
4	♂♎	2am00
5	☽♓	7pm13
7	☿♎	7am28
8	☽♈	5am02
8	☿♏	9pm42
10	☽♉	11am12
12	☽♊	2pm27
13	♀♑	2am14
14	☽♋	4pm21
16	☽♌	6pm19
18	☽♍	9pm15
21	☽♎	1am35
22	☉♐	0am19
23	☽♏	7am33
25	☽♐	3pm33
28	☽♑	1am57
30	☽♒	2pm26

DECEMBER

3	☽♓	3am23
3	☿♐	8pm26
5	☽♈	2pm17
7	☽♉	9pm27
8	♀♒	8am48
10	☽♊	0am50
12	☽♋	1am48
14	☽♌	2am09
16	☽♍	3am30
18	☽♎	7am01
20	☽♏	1pm12
21	☉♑	1pm37
22	☽♐	9pm57
23	☿♑	2am03
23	♂♏	2pm37
25	☽♑	8am54
27	☽♒	9pm25
30	☽♓	10am27

 (Figure 11)

LOCAL MEAN TIME OF SUNRISE FOR LATITUDES
60° North to 50° South

FOR ALL SUNDAYS IN 2000. (ALL TIMES ARE A.M.)

Date	LON-DON	60°	55°	50°	40°	30°	20°	10°	0°	10°	20°	30°	40°	50°
	H M	H M	H M	H M	H M	H M	H M	H M	H M	H M	H M	H M	H M	H M
1999 Dec. 26	8 5	9 4	8 25	7 58	7 20	6 54	6 32	6 14	5 57	5 39	5 20	4 58	4 30	3 50
2000 Jan. 2	8 6	9 2	8 25	7 58	7 22	6 56	6 35	6 17	6 0	5 43	5 24	5 2	4 35	3 55
9	8 4	8 57	8 21	7 57	7 22	6 57	6 37	6 19	6 3	5 46	5 29	5 8	4 41	4 3
16	8 0	8 48	8 16	7 53	7 20	6 57	6 38	6 22	6 6	5 50	5 33	5 13	4 49	4 13
23	7 52	8 35	8 7	7 46	7 16	6 55	6 38	6 22	6 8	5 54	5 38	5 20	4 57	4 25
30	7 43	8 21	7 56	7 38	7 11	6 52	6 37	6 23	6 9	5 56	5 42	5 26	5 5	4 37
Feb. 6	7 32	8 7	7 43	7 27	7 4	6 48	6 34	6 22	6 11	5 59	5 46	5 32	5 14	4 49
13	7 20	7 46	7 29	7 16	6 57	6 43	6 31	6 21	6 11	6 1	5 50	5 38	5 23	5 1
20	7 6	7 27	7 13	7 3	6 48	6 36	6 27	6 19	6 11	6 2	5 53	5 44	5 31	5 14
27	6 51	7 7	6 57	6 50	6 38	6 29	6 22	6 15	6 9	6 3	5 57	5 48	5 39	5 25
Mar. 5	6 36	6 47	6 40	6 35	6 27	6 22	6 17	6 12	6 8	6 4	5 59	5 54	5 47	5 37
12	6 21	6 26	6 23	6 20	6 16	6 14	6 11	6 9	6 7	6 4	6 1	5 59	5 54	5 49
19	6 5	6 5	6 5	6 5	6 5	6 5	6 5	6 5	6 4	6 4	6 4	6 3	6 2	6 0
26	5 49	5 44	5 47	5 50	5 54	5 57	5 59	6 1	6 2	6 4	6 5	6 7	6 9	6 11
Apr. 2	5 34	5 22	5 29	5 35	5 42	5 49	5 53	5 57	6 1	6 4	6 7	6 11	6 16	6 22
9	5 18	5 1	5 12	5 20	5 32	5 40	5 47	5 53	5 58	6 4	6 9	6 15	6 23	6 33
16	5 2	4 40	4 55	5 5	5 21	5 32	5 41	5 49	5 56	6 4	6 11	6 20	6 30	6 44
23	4 47	4 20	4 38	4 51	5 11	5 25	5 36	5 46	5 55	6 4	6 13	6 24	6 37	6 55
30	4 34	4 1	4 22	4 38	5 1	5 18	5 32	5 43	5 54	6 4	6 16	6 28	6 44	7 5
May 7	4 21	3 42	4 8	4 26	4 53	5 12	5 28	5 41	5 53	6 5	6 18	6 33	6 51	7 15
14	4 10	3 25	3 54	4 16	4 46	5 7	5 25	5 39	5 53	6 6	6 20	6 37	6 57	7 25
21	4 1	3 9	3 43	4 6	4 40	5 3	5 22	5 38	5 53	6 8	6 24	6 41	7 3	7 35
28	3 52	2 56	3 33	3 59	4 35	5 0	5 20	5 38	5 54	6 9	6 26	6 45	7 9	7 43
June 4	3 46	2 45	3 26	3 54	4 32	4 59	5 20	5 38	5 54	6 11	6 29	6·49	7 15	7 50
11	3 43	2 39	3 21	3 51	4 30	4 58	5 20	5 39	5 56	6 13	6 32	6 52	7 18	7 55
18	3 42	2 36	3 20	3 50	4 31	4 59	5 21	5 40	5 57	6 15	6 33	6 55	7 21	7 59
25	3 43	2 37	3 21	3 52	4 32	5 0	5 23	5 41	5 59	6 16	6 35	6 56	7 22	8 0
July 2	3 47	2 43	3 26	3 55	4 35	5 3	5 25	5 43	6 1	6 18	6 36	6 56	7 22	7 59
9	3 53	2 53	3 33	4 1	4 39	5 6	5 27	5 45	6 2	6 18	6 36	6 56	7 21	7 56
16	4 1	3 5	3 42	4 8	4 45	5 10	5 29	5 46	6 2	6 18	6 35	6 54	7 17	7 51
23	4 11	3 20	3 54	4 17	4 50	5 13	5 32	5 48	6 3	6 17	6 33	6 51	7 13	7 43
30	4 20	3 36	4 5	4 26	4 56	5 18	5 35	5 49	6 3	6 16	6 31	6 47	7 7	7 34
Aug. 6	4 31	3 52	4 18	4 36	5 3	5 22	5 37	5 50	6 2	6 15	6 27	6 41	6 59	7 23
13	4 42	4 9	4 31	4 46	5 9	5 26	5 39	5 51	6 1	6 12	6 23	6 36	6 50	7 12
20	4 53	4 26	4 44	4 57	5 16	5 30	5 41	5 51	6 0	6 9	6 18	6 29	6 41	6 59
27	5 5	4 43	4 47	5 7	5 23	5 34	5 43	5 51	5 58	6 5	6 12	6 21	6 31	6 45
Sept. 3	5 16	5 0	5 10	5 18	5 29	5 38	5 45	5 51	5 56	6 1	6 7	6 13	6 21	6 30
10	5 27	5 16	5 23	5 28	5 36	5 42	5 46	5 50	5 54	5 57	6 1	6 5	6 9	6 15
17	5 38	5 32	5 36	5 38	5 43	5 46	5 47	5 50	5 52	5 53	5 54	5 56	5 57	6 0
24	5 49	5 49	5 49	5 49	5 49	5 49	5 49	5 49	5 49	5 49	5 48	5 47	5 46	5 44
Oct. 1	6 1	6 5	6 3	6 0	5 56	5 53	5 51	5 49	5 46	5 44	5 42	5 39	5 35	5 29
8	6 12	6 22	6 16	6 11	6 3	5 58	5 52	5 48	5 45	5 40	5 35	5 30	5 23	5 14
15	6 23	6 39	6 30	6 22	6 11	6 2	5 55	5 48	5 42	5 36	5 30	5 22	5 13	4 59
22	6 36	6 57	6 43	6 33	6 18	6 7	5 57	5 49	5 41	5 33	5 25	5 15	5 2	4 45
29	6 49	7 15	6 57	6 45	6 25	6 12	6 0	5 50	5 40	5 31	5 20	5 8	4 53	4 32
Nov. 5	7 1	7 33	7 12	6 56	6 34	6 17	6 3	5 52	5 40	5 29	5 16	5 2	4 44	4 20
12	7 13	7 51	7 26	7 8	6 42	6 22	6 7	5 53	5 40	5 28	5 14	4 58	4 37	4 9
19	7 25	8 8	7 39	7 19	6 50	6 28	6 11	5 56	5 42	5 28	5 12	4 54	4 31	4 0
26	7 36	8 25	7 52	7 30	6 58	6 34	6 15	5 59	5 44	5 28	5 11	4 52	4 27	3 53
Dec. 3	7 46	8 39	8 4	7 39	7 5	6 40	6 20	6 3	5 46	5 30	5 12	4 51	4 25	3 48
10	7 55	8 50	8 14	7 47	7 11	6 45	6 25	6 6	5 49	5 32	5 13	4 52	4 25	3 45
17	8 1	8 59	8 20	7 53	7 15	6 49	6 28	6 10	5 53	5 35	5 16	4 54	4 26	3 46
24	8 4	9 3	8 24	7 57	7 20	6 53	6 32	6 13	5 56	5 38	5 19	4 57	4 29	3 49
31	8 3	9 3	8 25	7 58	7 22	6 55	6 34	6 16	6 0	5 43	5 24	5 2	4 34	3 54

Example:—To find the time of Sunrise in Jamaica (Latitude 18° N.) on Wednesday, June 21st, 2000. On June 18th, L.M.T.=5h. 21m.+$\frac{3}{10}\times$19m.=5h. 25m., on June 25th, L.M.T.=5h. 23m.+$\frac{3}{10}\times$18m.=5h. 27m., therefore L.M.T., on June 21st=5h. 25m.+$\frac{3}{7}\times$2m.=5h. 26m. A.M.

LOCAL MEAN TIME OF SUNSET FOR LATITUDES

60° North to 50° South

FOR ALL SUNDAYS IN 2000. (ALL TIMES ARE P.M.)

Date	NORTHERN LATITUDES								SOUTHERN LATITUDES					
	LONDON	60°	55°	50°	40°	30°	20°	10°	0°	10°	20°	30°	40°	50°
	H M	H M	H M	H M	H M	H M	H M	H M	H M	H M	H M	H M	H M	H M
1999 Dec. 26	3 55	2 57	3 36	4 3	4 41	5 7	5 28	5 47	6 4	6 22	6 40	7 2	7 30	8 11
2000 Jan. 2	4 2	3 5	3 43	4 9	4 46	5 12	5 32	5 50	6 7	6 25	6 43	7 5	7 32	8 12
9	4 10	3 17	3 53	4 17	4 52	5 17	5 37	5 54	6 10	6 27	6 45	7 6	7 32	8 9
16	4 20	3 32	4 4	4 27	4 59	5 23	5 41	5 58	6 13	6 29	6 46	7 5	7 30	8 5
23	4 31	3 49	4 17	4 38	5 7	5 29	5 46	6 1	6 15	6 30	6 45	7 3	7 26	7 58
30	4 44	4 7	4 31	4 50	5 15	5 35	5 50	6 4	6 17	6 30	6 44	7 0	7 20	7 49
Feb. 6	4 57	4 25	4 45	5 1	5 24	5 40	5 54	6 7	6 18	6 29	6 41	6 56	7 13	7 38
13	5 9	4 43	5 0	5 13	5 32	5 46	5 58	6 8	6 18	6 27	6 38	6 50	7 5	7 26
20	5 22	5 2	5 15	5 26	5 40	5 52	6 1	6 9	6 17	6 25	6 34	6 44	6 56	7 13
27	5 35	5 20	5 29	5 37	5 49	5 57	6 4	6 10	6 16	6 22	6 29	6 37	6 46	6 59
Mar. 5	5 47	5 38	5 44	5 49	5 56	6 2	6 7	6 11	6 15	6 19	6 24	6 29	6 36	6 45
12	5 59	5 55	5 58	6 1	6 4	6 7	6 9	6 11	6 13	6 15	6 18	6 21	6 24	6 30
19	6 11	6 12	6 12	6 11	6 11	6 11	6 11	6 11	6 11	6 11	6 12	6 12	6 13	6 14
26	6 23	6 29	6 26	6 23	6 18	6 15	6 13	6 11	6 9	6 7	6 6	6 4	6 2	5 59
Apr. 2	6 35	6 46	6 39	6 34	6 25	6 19	6 14	6 11	6 7	6 3	6 0	5 56	5 50	5 44
9	6 46	7 3	6 53	6 44	6 32	6 23	6 17	6 10	6 5	5 59	5 54	5 47	5 40	5 29
16	6 58	7 21	7 6	6 55	6 39	6 28	6 19	6 11	6 3	5 56	5 48	5 40	5 29	5 15
23	7 10	7 38	7 20	7 6	6 46	6 32	6 21	6 11	6 2	5 53	5 43	5 32	5 19	5 1
30	7 21	7 55	7 33	7 18	6 54	6 36	6 24	6 12	6 0	5 50	5 39	5 26	5 10	4 49
May 7	7 32	8 13	7 47	7 28	7 1	6 41	6 26	6 13	6 0	5 48	5 35	5 20	5 2	4 37
14	7 43	8 29	8 0	7 38	7 7	6 46	6 28	6 14	6 0	5 46	5 32	5 15	4 55	4 27
21	7 54	8 46	8 12	7 48	7 14	6 50	6 32	6 16	6 0	5 45	5 29	5 12	4 50	4 18
28	8 3	9 0	8 22	7 56	7 20	6 54	6 34	6 17	6 1	5 45	5 28	5 9	4 45	4 11
June 4	8 11	9 12	8 33	8 3	7 25	6 58	6 37	6 19	6 2	5 45	5 28	5 7	4 42	4 7
11	8 16	9 22	8 38	8 8	7 29	7 1	6 40	6 21	6 3	5 46	5 28	5 7	4 41	4 4
18	8 20	9 27	8 42	8 12	7 31	7 3	6 41	6 22	6 5	5 47	5 29	5 8	4 41	4 3
25	8 21	9 28	8 43	8 13	7 33	7 5	6 43	6 24	6 6	5 49	5 30	5 9	4 42	4 5
July 2	8 20	9 24	8 41	8 12	7 32	7 5	6 43	6 25	6 8	5 51	5 33	5 12	4 46	4 9
9	8 17	9 16	8 36	8 9	7 31	7 4	6 43	6 26	6 9	5 52	5 35	5 15	4 50	4 15
16	8 11	9 5	8 29	8 3	7 27	7 2	6 43	6 26	6 10	5 54	5 37	5 18	4 55	4 22
23	8 2	8 51	8 19	7 55	7 22	6 59	6 40	6 25	6 10	5 55	5 40	5 22	5 0	4 30
30	7 52	8 35	8 6	7 46	7 16	6 55	6 38	6 23	6 10	5 56	5 42	5 26	5 7	4 39
Aug. 6	7 40	8 17	7 53	7 34	7 8	6 49	6 34	6 22	6 9	5 57	5 44	5 31	5 13	4 48
13	7 28	7 59	7 38	7 22	6 59	6 43	6 30	6 18	6 8	5 58	5 47	5 34	5 19	4 59
20	7 13	7 39	7 22	7 9	6 50	6 36	6 25	6 16	6 7	5 58	5 49	5 38	5 26	5 9
27	6 58	7 18	7 5	6 55	6 39	6 28	6 19	6 12	6 5	5 58	5 50	5 42	5 32	5 19
Sept. 3	6 43	6 58	6 47	6 40	6 29	6 20	6 14	6 8	6 2	5 57	5 52	5 46	5 39	5 29
10	6 27	6 36	6 30	6 25	6 17	6 12	6 7	6 4	6 0	5 57	5 54	5 50	5 45	5 39
17	6 11	6 15	6 12	6 9	6 5	6 3	6 1	5 59	5 58	5 56	5 55	5 54	5 52	5 50
24	5 55	5 54	5 54	5 54	5 54	5 54	5 55	5 55	5 55	5 56	5 57	5 57	5 58	6 0
Oct. 1	5 38	5 33	5 36	5 39	5 43	5 46	5 48	5 51	5 53	5 55	5 58	6 1	6 5	6 11
8	5 23	5 12	5 18	5 24	5 31	5 38	5 42	5 47	5 51	5 55	6 0	6 6	6 12	6 22
15	5 8	4 51	5 1	5 9	5 21	5 29	5 37	5 43	5 49	5 55	6 2	6 10	6 20	6 33
22	4 53	4 31	4 44	4 55	5 11	5 22	5 32	5 40	5 48	5 56	6 5	6 15	6 27	6 45
29	4 39	4 12	4 29	4 42	5 2	5 15	5 27	5 38	5 47	5 57	6 8	6 20	6 35	6 57
Nov. 5	4 27	3 54	4 15	4 31	4 53	5 10	5 24	5 36	5 47	5 59	6 11	6 25	6 44	7 8
12	4 16	3 37	4 2	4 20	4 46	5 6	5 21	5 35	5 48	6 1	6 15	6 31	6 52	7 21
19	4 6	3 22	3 51	4 11	4 41	5 3	5 20	5 35	5 49	6 3	6 19	6 37	7 0	7 32
26	3 58	3 10	3 42	4 5	4 37	5 0	5 19	5 36	5 51	6 7	6 23	6 43	7 8	7 43
Dec. 3	3 53	3 0	3 35	4 0	4 35	5 0	5 20	5 37	5 54	6 10	6 28	6 49	7 15	7 53
10	3 51	2 55	3 32	3 58	4 35	5 1	5 21	5 39	5 57	6 14	6 33	6 54	7 22	8 1
17	3 52	2 53	3 32	3 59	4 37	5 3	5 24	5 43	6 0	6 18	6 36	6 58	7 26	8 7
24	3 55	2 56	3 35	4 2	4 40	5 6	5 27	5 46	6 3	6 21	6 40	7 2	7 30	8 11
31	4 1	3 3	3 41	4 8	4 45	5 11	5 32	5 49	6 6	6 24	6 42	7 4	7 32	8 12

Example:—To find the time of Sunset in Canberra (Latitude 35°.3S.) on Thursday, August 3rd, 2000. On July 30th, L.M.T.=5h. 26m.−$\frac{7}{10}$×19m.=5h. 16m., on August 6th, L.M.T.=5h. 31m.−$\frac{3}{10}$×18m.=5h. 21m., therefore L.M.T. on August 3rd=5h. 16m.+$\frac{3}{7}$×5m.=5h. 19m. P.M.

TABLES OF HOUSES FOR LONDON, Latitude 51° 32' N.

Upper section — Table 1

Sidereal Time (H. M. S.)	10 ♈	11 ♉	12 ♊	Ascen ♋	2 ♌	3 ♍
0 0 0	0	9	22	26 36	12	3
0 3 40	1	10	23	27 17	13	3
0 7 20	2	11	24	27 56	14	4
0 11 0	3	12	25	28 42	15	5
0 14 41	4	13	25	29 17	15	6
0 18 21	5	14	26	29 55	16	7
0 22 2	6	15	27	0Ω34	17	8
0 25 42	7	16	28	1 14	18	8
0 29 23	8	17	29	1 55	18	9
0 33 4	9	18	69	2 33	19	10
0 36 45	10	19	1	3 14	20	11
0 40 26	11	20	1	3 54	20	12
0 44 8	12	21	2	4 33	21	13
0 47 50	13	22	3	5 12	22	14
0 51 32	14	23	4	5 52	23	15
0 55 14	15	24	5	6 30	23	15
0 58 57	16	25	6	7 9	24	16
1 2 40	17	26	6	7 50	25	17
1 6 23	18	27	7	8 30	26	18
1 10 7	19	28	8	9 9	26	19
1 13 51	20	29	9	9 48	27	19
1 17 35	21	♊	10	10 28	28	20
1 21 20	22	1	10	11 8	28	21
1 25 6	23	2	11	11 48	29	22
1 28 52	24	3	12	12 28	mp	23
1 32 38	25	4	13	13 8	1	24
1 36 25	26	5	14	13 48	1	25
1 40 12	27	6	14	14 28	2	25
1 44 0	28	7	15	15 8	3	26
1 47 48	29	8	16	15 48	4	27
1 51 37	30	9	17	16 28	4	28

Upper section — Table 2

Sidereal Time (H. M. S.)	10 ♉	11 ♊	12 ♋	Ascen ♌	2 ♍	3 ♍
1 51 37	0	9	17	16 28	4	28
1 55 27	1	10	18	17 8	5	29
1 59 17	2	11	19	17 48	6	♎
2 3 8	3	12	19	18 28	7	1
2 6 59	4	13	20	19 9	8	2
2 10 51	5	14	21	19 49	9	2
2 14 44	6	15	22	20 29	9	3
2 18 37	7	16	22	21 10	10	4
2 22 31	8	17	23	21 51	11	5
2 26 25	9	18	24	22 32	11	6
2 30 20	10	19	25	23 14	12	7
2 34 16	11	20	25	23 55	13	8
2 38 13	12	21	26	24 36	14	9
2 42 10	13	22	27	25 17	15	10
2 46 8	14	23	28	25 58	15	11
2 50 7	15	24	29	26 40	16	12
2 54 7	16	25	29	27 22	17	12
2 58 7	17	26	Ω	28 4	18	13
3 2 8	18	27	1	28 46	18	14
3 6 9	19	27	2	29 28	19	15
3 10 12	20	28	3	0mp12	20	16
3 14 15	21	29	3	0 54	21	17
3 18 19	22	69	4	1 36	22	18
3 22 23	23	1	5	2 20	22	19
3 26 29	24	2	6	3 2	23	20
3 30 35	25	3	7	3 45	24	21
3 34 41	26	4	7	4 28	25	22
3 38 49	27	5	8	5 11	26	23
3 42 57	28	6	9	5 54	27	24
3 47 6	29	7	10	6 38	27	25
3 51 15	30	8	11	7 21	28	25

Upper section — Table 3

Sidereal Time (H. M. S.)	10 ♊	11 ♋	12 ♌	Ascen ♍	2 ♍	3 ♎
3 51 15	0	8	11	7 21	28	25
3 55 25	1	9	12	8 5	29	26
3 59 36	2	10	12	8 49	♎	27
4 3 48	3	10	13	9 33	1	28
4 8 0	4	11	14	10 17	2	29
4 12 13	5	12	15	11 2	2	m
4 16 26	6	13	16	11 46	3	1
4 20 40	7	14	17	12 30	4	2
4 24 55	8	15	17	13 15	5	3
4 29 10	9	16	18	14 0	6	4
4 33 26	10	17	19	14 45	7	5
4 37 42	11	18	20	15 30	8	6
4 41 59	12	19	21	16 15	8	7
4 46 16	13	20	21	17 0	9	8
4 50 34	14	21	22	17 45	10	9
4 54 52	15	22	23	18 30	11	10
4 59 10	16	23	24	19 16	12	11
5 3 29	17	24	25	20 3	13	12
5 7 49	18	25	26	20 49	14	13
5 12 9	19	25	27	21 35	14	14
5 16 29	20	26	28	22 20	15	14
5 20 49	21	27	28	23 6	16	15
5 25 9	22	28	29	23 51	16	16
5 29 30	23	29	mp	24 37	18	17
5 33 51	24	Ω	1	25 23	19	18
5 38 12	25	1	2	26 9	20	19
5 42 34	26	2	3	26 55	21	20
5 46 55	27	3	4	27 41	21	21
5 51 17	28	4	4	28 27	22	22
5 55 38	29	5	5	29 13	23	23
6 0 0	30	6	6	30 0	24	24

Lower section — Table 1

Sidereal Time (H. M. S.)	10 ♋	11 ♌	12 ♍	Ascen ♎	2 ♎	3 ♏
6 0 0	0	6	6	0 0	24	24
6 4 22	1	7	7	0 47	25	25
6 8 43	2	8	8	1 33	26	26
6 13 5	3	9	9	2 19	27	27
6 17 26	4	10	10	3 5	27	28
6 21 48	5	11	10	3 51	28	29
6 26 9	6	12	11	4 37	29	♐
6 30 30	7	13	12	5 23	m	1
6 34 51	8	14	13	6 9	1	2
6 39 11	9	15	14	6 55	2	3
6 43 31	10	16	15	7 40	2	4
6 47 51	11	16	16	8 26	3	4
6 52 11	12	17	16	9 12	4	5
6 56 31	13	18	17	9 58	5	6
7 0 50	14	19	18	10 43	6	7
7 5 8	15	20	19	11 28	7	8
7 9 26	16	21	20	12 14	8	9
7 13 44	17	22	21	12 59	8	10
7 18 1	18	23	22	13 45	9	11
7 22 18	19	24	23	14 30	10	12
7 26 34	20	25	24	15 15	11	13
7 30 50	21	26	25	16 0	12	14
7 35 5	22	27	25	16 45	13	15
7 39 20	23	28	26	17 30	13	16
7 43 34	24	29	27	18 15	14	17
7 47 47	25	mp	28	18 59	15	18
7 52 0	26	1	29	19 43	16	19
7 56 12	27	2	29	20 27	17	20
8 0 24	28	3	♎	21 11	18	20
8 4 35	29	4	1	21 56	18	21
8 8 45	30	5	2	22 40	19	22

Lower section — Table 2

Sidereal Time (H. M. S.)	10 ♌	11 ♍	12 ♎	Ascen ♎	2 ♏	3 ♐
8 8 45	0	5	2	22 40	19	22
8 12 54	1	5	3	23 24	20	23
8 17 3	2	6	3	24 7	21	24
8 21 11	3	7	4	24 50	22	25
8 25 19	4	8	5	25 34	23	26
8 29 26	5	9	6	26 18	23	27
8 33 31	6	10	7	27 1	24	28
8 37 37	7	11	8	27 44	25	29
8 41 41	8	12	8	28 26	26	vs
8 45 45	9	13	9	29 8	27	1
8 49 48	10	14	10	29 50	27	2
8 53 51	11	15	11	0m32	28	3
8 57 52	12	16	12	1 15	29	4
9 1 53	13	17	12	1 58	♐	5
9 5 53	14	18	13	2 39	1	6
9 9 53	15	18	14	3 21	1	6
9 13 52	16	19	15	4 3	2	7
9 17 50	17	20	16	4 44	3	8
9 21 47	18	21	16	5 26	3	9
9 25 44	19	22	17	6 7	4	10
9 29 40	20	23	18	6 48	5	11
9 33 35	21	24	18	7 29	5	12
9 37 29	22	25	19	8 9	6	13
9 41 23	23	26	20	8 50	7	14
9 45 16	24	27	21	9 31	8	15
9 49 9	25	28	22	10 11	9	16
9 53 1	26	28	23	10 51	9	17
9 56 52	27	29	23	11 32	10	18
10 0 43	28	♎	24	12 12	11	19
10 4 33	29	1	25	12 53	12	20
10 8 23	30	2	26	13 33	13	20

Lower section — Table 3

Sidereal Time (H. M. S.)	10 ♍	11 ♎	12 ♎	Ascen ♏	2 ♐	3 vs
10 8 23	0	2	26	13 33	13	20
10 12 12	1	3	26	14 13	14	21
10 16 0	2	4	27	14 53	15	22
10 19 48	3	5	28	15 33	15	23
10 23 35	4	5	29	16 13	16	24
10 27 22	5	6	29	16 52	17	25
10 31 8	6	7	m	17 32	18	26
10 34 54	7	8	1	18 12	19	27
10 38 40	8	9	2	18 52	20	28
10 42 25	9	10	2	19 31	20	29
10 46 9	10	11	3	20 11	21	≈
10 49 53	11	11	4	20 50	22	1
10 53 37	12	12	4	21 30	23	2
10 57 20	13	13	5	22 9	24	3
11 1 3	14	14	6	22 49	24	4
11 4 46	15	15	7	23 28	25	5
11 8 28	16	16	7	24 8	26	6
11 12 10	17	17	8	24 47	27	8
11 15 52	18	17	9	25 27	28	9
11 19 34	19	18	10	26 6	29	10
11 23 15	20	19	10	26 45	vs	11
11 26 56	21	20	11	27 25	0	12
11 30 37	22	21	12	28 5	1	13
11 34 18	23	22	13	28 44	2	14
11 37 58	24	23	13	29 24	3	15
11 41 39	25	23	14	0♐ 3	4	16
11 45 19	26	24	15	0 43	5	17
11 49 0	27	25	15	1 23	6	18
11 52 40	28	26	16	2 3	6	19
11 56 20	29	27	17	2 43	7	20
12 0 0	30	27	17	3 23	8	21

Conversion of Longitude to Time

Degrees	h	m	Degrees	h	m	Degrees	h	m	Degrees	h	m
0	0	00	45	3	00	90	6	00	135	9	00
1	0	04	46	3	04	91	6	04	136	9	04
2	0	08	47	3	08	92	6	08	137	9	08
3	0	12	48	3	12	93	6	12	138	9	12
4	0	16	49	3	16	94	6	16	139	9	16
5	0	20	50	3	20	95	6	20	140	9	20
6	0	24	51	3	24	96	6	24	141	9	24
7	0	28	52	3	28	97	6	28	142	9	28
8	0	32	53	3	32	98	6	32	143	9	32
9	0	36	54	3	36	99	6	36	144	9	36
10	0	40	55	3	40	100	6	40	145	9	40
11	0	44	56	3	44	101	6	44	146	9	44
12	0	48	57	3	48	102	6	48	147	9	48
13	0	52	58	3	52	103	6	52	148	9	52
14	0	56	59	3	56	104	6	56	149	9	56
15	1	00	60	4	00	105	7	00	150	10	00
16	1	04	61	4	04	106	7	04	151	10	04
17	1	08	62	4	08	107	7	08	152	10	08
18	1	12	63	4	12	108	7	12	153	10	12
19	1	16	64	4	16	109	7	16	154	10	16
20	1	20	65	4	20	110	7	20	155	10	20
21	1	24	66	4	24	111	7	24	156	10	24
22	1	28	67	4	28	112	7	28	157	10	28
23	1	32	68	4	32	113	7	32	158	10	32
24	1	36	69	4	36	114	7	36	159	10	36
25	1	40	70	4	40	115	7	40	160	10	40
26	1	44	71	4	44	116	7	44	161	10	44
27	1	48	72	4	48	117	7	48	162	10	48
28	1	52	73	4	52	118	7	52	163	10	52
29	1	56	74	4	56	119	7	56	164	10	56
30	2	00	75	5	00	120	8	00	165	11	00
31	2	04	76	5	04	121	8	04	166	11	04
32	2	08	77	5	08	122	8	08	167	11	08
33	2	12	78	5	12	123	8	12	168	11	12
34	2	16	79	5	16	124	8	16	169	11	16
35	2	20	80	5	20	125	8	20	170	11	20
36	2	24	81	5	24	126	8	24	171	11	24
37	2	28	82	5	28	127	8	28	172	11	28
38	2	32	83	5	32	128	8	32	173	11	32
39	2	36	84	5	36	129	8	36	174	11	36
40	2	40	85	5	40	130	8	40	175	11	40
41	2	44	86	5	44	131	8	44	176	11	44
42	2	48	87	5	48	132	8	48	177	11	48
43	2	52	88	5	52	133	8	52	178	11	52
44	2	56	89	5	56	134	8	56	179	11	56

Figure 15

Daylight Saving Time Information

1880 GMT	**1932** April 17 GMT + 1 h	**1948** March 14 GMT + 1 h	**1966** March 20 GMT + 1 h	**1986** March 30 GMT + 1 h
1916 May 21 GMT + 1 h	**1932** October 2 GMT	**1948** October 31 GMT	**1966** October 23 GMT	**1986** October 26 GMT
1916 October 1 GMT	**1933** April 9 GMT + 1 h	**1949** April 3 GMT + 1 h	**1967** March 19 GMT + 1 h	**1987** March 29 GMT + 1 h
1917 April 8 GMT + 1 h	**1933** October 8 GMT	**1949** October 30 GMT	**1967** October 29 GMT	**1987** October 25 GMT
1917 September 30 GMT	**1934** April 22 GMT + 1 h	**1950** April 16 GMT + 1 h	**1968** February 18 GMT + 1 h	**1988** March 27 GMT + 1 h
1918 March 24 GMT + 1 h	**1934** October 7 GMT	**1950** October 22 GMT	**1971** October 31 GMT	**1988** October 23 GMT
1918 September 30 GMT	**1935** April 14 GMT + 1 h	**1951** April 15 GMT + 1 h	**1972** March 19 GMT + 1 h	**1989** March 26 GMT + 1 h
1919 March 30 GMT + 1 h	**1935** October 6 GMT	**1951** October 21 GMT	**1972** October 29 GMT	**1989** October 29 GMT
1919 September 29 GMT	**1936** April 19 GMT + 1 h	**1952** April 20 GMT + 1 h	**1973** March 18 GMT + 1 h	**1990** March 25 GMT + 1 h
1920 March 28 GMT + 1 h	**1936** October 4 GMT	**1952** October 26 GMT	**1973** October 28 GMT	**1990** October 28 GMT
1920 October 25 GMT	**1937** April 18 GMT + 1 h	**1953** April 19 GMT + 1 h	**1974** March 17 GMT + 1 h	**1991** March 31 GMT + 1 h
1921 April 3 GMT + 1 h	**1937** October 3 GMT	**1953** October 4 GMT	**1974** October 27 GMT	**1991** October 27 GMT
1921 October 3 GMT	**1938** April 10 GMT + 1 h	**1954** April 11 GMT + 1 h	**1975** March 16 GMT + 1 h	**1992** March 29 GMT + 1 h
1922 March 26 GMT + 1 h	**1938** October 2 GMT	**1954** October 3 GMT	**1975** October 26 GMT	**1992** October 25 GMT
1922 October 8 GMT	**1939** April 16 GMT + 1 h	**1955** April 17 GMT + 1 h	**1976** March 21 GMT + 1 h	**1993** March 28 GMT + 1 h
1923 April 22 GMT + 1 h	**1939** November 19 GMT	**1955** October 2 GMT	**1976** October 24 GMT	**1993** October 24 GMT
1923 September 16 GMT	**1940** February 25 GMT + 1 h	**1956** April 22 GMT + 1 h	**1977** March 20 GMT + 1 h	**1994** March 27 GMT + 1 h
1924 April 13 GMT + 1 h	**1941** May 4 GMT + 2 h	**1956** October 7 GMT	**1977** October 23 GMT	**1994** October 23 GMT
1924 September 21 GMT	**1941** August 10 GMT + 1h	**1958** April 20 GMT + 1 h	**1978** March 19 GMT + 1 h	**1995** March 25 GMT + 1 h
1925 April 19 GMT + 1 h	**1942** April 5 GMT + 2 h	**1958** October 5 GMT	**1978** October 29 GMT	**1995** October 22 GMT
1925 October 4 GMT	**1942** August 9 GMT + 1 h	**1959** April 19 GMT + 1 h	**1979** March 18 GMT + 1 h	**1996** March 31 GMT + 1 h
1926 April 18 GMT + 1 h	**1943** April 4 GMT + 2 h	**1959** October 4 GMT	**1979** October 28 GMT	**1996** October 27 GMT
1926 October 3 GMT	**1943** August 15 GMT + 1 h	**1960** April 10 GMT + 1 h	**1980** March 16 GMT + 1 h	**1997** March 30 GMT + 1 h
1927 April 10 GMT + 1 h	**1944** April 2 GMT + 2 h	**1960** October 2 GMT	**1980** October 26 GMT	**1997** October 26 GMT
1927 October 2 GMT	**1944** September 17 GMT + 1 h	**1961** March 26 GMT + 1 h	**1981** March 29 GMT + 1 h	**1998** March 29 GMT + 1 h
1928 April 22 GMT + 1 h	**1945** April 2 GMT + 2 h	**1961** October 29 GMT	**1981** October 25 GMT	**1998** October 25 GMT
1928 Oct 7 GMT	**1945** July 15 GMT + 1 h	**1962** March 25 GMT + 1 h	**1982** March 28 GMT + 1 h	**1999** March 28 GMT + 1 h
1929 April 21 GMT + 1 h	**1945** October 7 GMT	**1962** October 28 GMT	**1982** October 24 GMT	**1999** October 31 GMT
1929 October 6 GMT	**1946** April 14 GMT + 1 h	**1963** March 31 GMT + 1 h	**1983** March 27 GMT + 1 h	**2000** March 16 GMT + 1 h
1930 April 13 GMT + 1h	**1946** October 6 GMT	**1963** October 27 GMT	**1983** October 23 GMT	**2000** October 29 GMT
1930 October 5 GMT	**1947** March 16 GMT + 1 h	**1964** March 22 GMT + 1 h	**1984** March 25 GMT + 1h	**2001** March 25 GMT + 1 h
1931 April 19 GMT + 1h	**1947** April 13 GMT + 2 h	**1964** October 25 GMT	**1984** October 28 GMT	**2001** October 28 GMT
1931 October 4 GMT	**1947** August 10 GMT + 1 h	**1965** March 21 GMT + 1 h	**1985** March 31 GMT + 1 h	
	1947 November 2 GMT	**1965** October 24 GMT	**1985** October 27 GMT	

Figure 16

94

Index